the working electron

a library of practical programs

john scriven

All programs are compatible with the BBC micro.

First published 1984 by:
Sunshine Books (an imprint of Scot Press Ltd.)
12–13 Little Newport Street
London WC2R 3LD

British Library Cataloguing in Publication Data

Scriven, John
    The Working Electron.
    1. Electron (Computer)—Programming
    I. Title
    001.64'25   QA76.8.E/

ISBN 0-946408-52-1

Cover design by Grad Graphic Design Ltd.
Cover illustration by Stuart Hughes.
Typeset by Paragon Photoset, Aylesbury.
Printed in Great Britain by Short Run Press Ltd, Exeter.

CONTENTS

Contents in detail

Introduction

The structure of the book — modules and procedures — entering the programs — use of LISTO7 and WIDTH40 — useful hints and tips.

CHAPTER 1

Information Handling

Methods of storing data — cardboxes and data — particular problems with Acorn machines — Garbage and Dustman — files, cassettes and disks — ordering the files — PROC_save and PROC_load: file transfer — Number: a program to show binary chopping — Defined Function Conversion: a program to convert lower to upper case — Binary Sort: a program showing a typical binary search procedure.

CHAPTER 2

The Domestic Servant

Detailing home expenses — annual expenditure and monthly analysis — menus and flags — Car Log: a program to evaluate running a car — efficient methods for storing and sorting data — storing at bit, rather than byte, level — home databases — computers in the kitchen — Chef: a program to make meal preparation easier — the computer as secretary — Texted: a program to produce and store standard letters.

CHAPTER 3

Characters and Plots in Display

How the display is achieved on the screen — letters and numbers — Character View: a program to see in detail how characters are stored — Define New Characters: defining your own alphabet — Character Rotate: a program to produce sideways letters — Character Designer: building a good character — extended graphics — different plots — saving commands — Sketch: a different way to save screen art — Design: an easy-to-use graphics design package.

CHAPTER 4
Down to Business
Valid programs — home accounts — flexibility in design versus purpose-built software — Accounts: a program to record expenditure or income and present the results in a variety of forms — business diaries and appointment systems — methods for coding days of the week — ordered information — Diary: a program that acts as a mini personal database — more on display — different forms of graphs and charts — Unigraph: a universal graph program to provide block graphs and pie charts from a variety of information.

CHAPTER 5
The Crystal Ball
Statistics and misinformation — means, variance, samples and distribution — Elementary Stats: a program to calculate simple statistical results — chances and probability — predicting the future — lines of best fit — Linear Projections: a program to calculate how well data fits on a linear graph and what form future trends might take.

CHAPTER 6
Home Education
Education and learning — useful and not-so-useful programs — Quiz: a universal quiz program that allows you to make up and use quizzes in any subject — learning maths — diversionary tactics — Boris: a program to perform multiplications the really long way — binary thoughts — keyboard skills, typewriters and computers — Typist: a program to help improve your keyboard skills in graduated steps — Sound Demo: a program to alter parameters of SOUND and ENVELOPE — Music in Data: a program which stores notes as data statements — Synth: a program to teach piano notes and written music as well as turning the computer into a musical instrument.

CHAPTER 7
Program Design
Design philosophy — readable programs — structure in BBC BASIC — variable and procedure names — writing your own programs — Stock: an example program to store customer information in different areas — how modules can be built up — number formatting — program debugging.

Program Notes

The programs included in this book are intended for the Electron computer, but they will all work on the BBC micro. In some cases, lines have been added which will not affect the Electron, but which will make use of the additional facilities of the BBC.

The ^ sign used throughout the program listings is the exponential sign.

Before entering the programs, read the section called 'Entering the programs' in the Introduction, which explains the layout of the program lines.

Introduction

In 1981, Acorn Computers revealed the BBC microcomputer. It was acclaimed immediately as one of the best-equipped machines on the market, with an excellent BASIC and a wide range of different interfaces, enabling it to be connected to a variety of peripheral devices. Under the Department of Industry scheme, most schools in the UK equipped themselves with at least one BBC micro, and BBC BASIC has become the standard educational BASIC.

Two years later, the Electron appeared at half the price, offering the same BASIC and operating system, with only a slight reduction in speed and without some of the interfaces. BBC BASIC is one of the best on the market containing some very advanced features, and recent manufacturers have copied many of these. When the Electron was manufactured, this excellent language became available to even more people.

These two computers offer home and business users a wealth of facilities that can turn the computers into games machines, word-processors, music synthesizers and data-processors. There are several books available that show you how to turn your micro into a game machine, but even the most hardened arcade addict will realise that there is more to a computer than zapping aliens. Contained within these pages is a collection of programs that show how the Acorn machines can be put to some serious uses in a wide range of fields, although 'serious' is not meant to imply dull.

The structure of this book

This book does not aim to teach you BASIC: there are enough publications available for that purpose. It is aimed at users who have a limited knowledge of BASIC, but who want to extend their skills in different directions. It covers a wide range of applications to which Acorn computers can be put, including data storage, finance, graphics, sound, music, household management and education. The text contains discussion of the programming techniques involved, but this is not presented in a formal 'learn this' manner. It *is* possible simply to type in the programs as they are written — indeed, this book contains more than 20 programs, and just one commercial program costs a lot more than the price of this book — but the intention is that you will modify the programs, and it is hoped that, in doing so, you will improve your knowledge of programming.

The previous books in this series, written by my friend David Lawrence, have all used a modular approach. In other words, they are written in separate modules or sections. Each section of code serves some specific purpose and can be used in other programs. BBC BASIC cries out to be used in this fashion, with its procedures and defined functions, so it was easy for me to keep within the spirit of David's books.

The programs are fully annotated, so they should be fairly easy to understand. As far as possible, I have used the convention of long variable names in lower case and reserved upper case for BASIC words, eg numberofcakes = 6 and name$ = "Fred".

The exceptions are loop variables and coordinates, eg

FOR N = 1 TO 10 *and* X% = 100

Procedures usually have meaningful names such as PROC_shoot, and BBC BASIC allows you to test these as they are written, without the need to enter the whole program. You can shorten variable names if you wish, and the programs may run faster, especially if you use integer variables where possible, eg

AX% = 10 *instead of* distancemoved = 10

You may also find that it is quicker to enter programs by using the single key function on the Electron, or the abbreviated form if you are using a BBC micro, eg hold the <CAPS LK/FUNC> down while pressing L or simply enter L. instead of LIST. There are frequent occasions when lines are very similar, and judicious use of the COPY key can save a lot of typing. Another convention I have adopted is to use angular brackets when a particular key is being referred to, eg press <RETURN> refers to the key marked RETURN.

Entering the programs

My main aim has been to show how the programs work rather than to produce zippy programs that are difficult to understand. Above all, this is not a book merely for reading, but for reading and using. No-one ever developed programming skills from books alone, and the best way to become more familiar with your computer is by entering these programs and adapting them to your own use. In many areas, we learn more from making mistakes, gaining skills as we correct the errors. This is especially true in computing, and a lot of the fun (and, it must be admitted, the frustration!) comes from finding out why your programs fail to work in the way you expect.

It is to be hoped, of course, that many of the ideas you glean from this book will help speed up your program-writing and prevent most of the more common errors, but very few programs are completely bug-free. When something doesn't work, don't give up; go for a walk and come back to the problem, and it can often be solved.

The listings in this book have all been dumped from working programs straight to a printer. Occasionally, even this is not completely fool-proof, but it is unlikely that the programs contained within will fail to work. In order to make the listings clear, they have been printed after setting the print width to a particular size (WIDTH40), so that the listings fit across the page. In some programs with long lines this has meant that lines are split awkwardly, although I have tried to avoid this. If you are copying them in, don't press (RETURN) until you reach the next line number. As an example, if you see a line in the book:

```
1010 IF A% > B% AND C% < D% THEN PRINT
     Z$ ELSE PRINT Y$
```

then this would be entered as

```
1010 IF A% > B% AND C% < D% THEN PRINT Z$ ELSE PRINT Y$
```

If you enter this line as instructed, enter LISTO7, then WIDTH40 and then LIST 1010, you will see the computer sets out the line as in example A. You will need seven spaces after the word PRINT to get the line exactly right (two on the first line and five on the second).

The command LISTO7 (list option 7) has also been used to indent loops. This means that it appears as if there are a lot of spaces in the listings, eg

```
1000 REPEAT
1010     Z$=GET$
1020     UNTIL Z$ = "Y"
```

These spaces are inserted by the computer in the LISTOption mode and are designed to make the structure of loops clearer. They are not necessary to make the programs work, and those spaces between line numbers and the instructions should be ignored when entering the programs. They will appear automatically if you enter the LISTOption, eg

1000PRINT "HELLO" will appear as
1000 PRINT "HELLO"

after using LISTO with numbers greater than zero. LISTO followed by zero switches off the indentation and removes the spaces. Use this mode when entering programs so you don't put extra spaces in, when using the <COPY> key.

Spaces between words are usually optional but look out for the TAB command.

PRINTTAB(2,3) is permissible.
PRINTTAB (2,3) will stop the program with a 'No such variable' message.

This is explained in more detail later on. Remember that full stops and commas are important, as is the difference between colons and semi-colons. Incidentally, program lines with nothing after them can be achieved by pressing the space bar before (RETURN). They serve no purpose other than breaking up the program.

These are the sort of things to look out for, but you will soon find that you know what looks right in BBC BASIC. Many of the programs are used regularly both by myself and others, and I hope that they give you as much pleasure in use as writing them gave me.

CHAPTER 1
Information Handling

Methods of storing data

Many of the programs in this book rely on their ability to store and manipulate information. It is important to consider the ways in which this information can be loaded into the computer in the first place. It can be entered from the keyboard each time the program is run, stored permanently in the form of variables, held in data statements, or it can be loaded in from tape or disk. Here are examples of the first three methods.

1 Entering from the keyboard.

```
10 INPUT "ENTER A NUMBER"number
20 INPUT "ENTER YOUR NAME"name$
30 PRINT name$" ENTERED "number
```

2 Constants held as variables.

```
10 cabbage = 20
20 INPUT "HOW MANY CABBAGES?"number
30 price = number * cabbages
40 PRINT "YOU MUST PAY "price" PENCE"
```

3 Values held in data statements.

```
10 INPUT "ENTER THE DAY NUMBER"daynum
20 RESTORE
30 FOR N = 1 TO daynum
40 READ day$
50 PRINT "THE DAY IS "day$
60 DATA SUNDAY, MONDAY, TUESDAY
70 DATA WEDNESDAY, THURSDAY, FRIDAY
80 DATA SATURDAY
```

There are drawbacks in all these methods. Information entered at the keyboard is very time-consuming, and constants and data statements cannot be altered unless the program itself is changed. The usual way of supplying the computer with changing data is by using data files. The framework of the program remains the same, which means that it can often be used for many purposes. It is a little like using a cardbox system in an office or the home.

When you buy a cardbox, it contains no information, and all the cards are blank. It is up to you whether you fill it with information on customers, a list of recipes or details of your stamp collection. In this respect, it would be possible to design a universal database program that is like an empty cardbox. There are drawbacks to this sort of approach, however. Suppose you use the database to store information on stamps. You might want to keep records on hundreds of stamps, but only need to store their country of origin, their value and date of issue. In another program, you might want to store just a few records, but each one containing detailed information.

Both the Electron and the BBC machines contain complex operating systems that together with BASIC take up 32K. As the 6502 processor can address 64K, there is only 32K left for RAM. After some of this has been used for the screen display, there is only a limited amount of memory remaining. If you deduct the space occupied by the program itself, there is often less than 10K on the Electron in MODE 6, and less than 15K in MODE 7 on the BBC. This is an important consideration when designing programs, as it is easy to run out of memory space when using large arrays, particularly those containing strings.

If you think of string variables as being little 'boxes' that contain the strings, then each time the box changes its string, the former contents do not magically disappear into thin air. They continue to take up variable space, and eventually you will run out of memory. In some computers, there is an internal housekeeping routine that handles the discarded extra copies of variables. Because this is like the dustmen coming round each week, it is known as garbage collection. This does not happen in Acorn machines, as the following example will demonstrate.

Garbage

```
1000 REM  **   GARBAGE   **
1010
1020 MODE1
1030
1040
1050
1060
1070 A$=" "
1080 B$=" "
1090 C$=" "
1100 D$=" "
```

```
1110 FOR N = 1 TO 255
1120    A$ = A$+"*"
1130    B$ = B$+"B"
1140    C$ = C$+"C"
1150    D$ = D$+"D"
1160    NEXT N
1170 PRINT A$, B$, C$, D$
```

Although you are only dealing with four variables, and you might imagine they would only take up about 1K (4 * 255), you will find you get an out of memory message — No room at line x. If you type in PRINT N, you will discover how far the program has progressed. This should demonstrate how careful you need to be when designing programs. You can get round this situation, however, with a little planning. If you know at the start of the program the maximum size of the variables, then you can reserve space for them by filling them with any characters, then emptying them. If you try the next program, then you will see that the only difference is that it contains four extra lines to fill out the variable space, then empty it. If you run this program, you will find you don't run out of memory.

Dustman

```
1000 REM  **  DUSTMAN  **
1010
1020 MODE1
1030 A$ = STRING$(255,"*")
1040 B$ = STRING$(255,"*")
1050 C$ = STRING$(255,"*")
1060 D$ = STRING$(255,"*")
1070 A$=""
1080 B$=""
1090 C$=""
1100 D$=""
1110 FOR N = 1 TO 255
1120    A$ = A$+"*"
1130    B$ = B$+"B"
1140    C$ = C$+"C"
1150    D$ = D$+"D"
1160    NEXT N
1170 PRINT A$, B$, C$, D$
```

Files and things

In the world of computers, the word 'file' covers a variety of types of information. A program is a file, so is the display on the screen and so is the collection of variables to be manipulated in the program. It is the latter case that is being considered here, and there are a few more terms that need to be explained.

If you imagine a telephone directory, then the whole book constitutes a file. Each entry is called a record, and this can be split up into separate sections called fields.

File: Bristol telephone directory.
Record 1: A Aardvark, 2 High St Clifton, BRISTOL 123456

Record 1 contains three fields:

Name: A Aardvark
Address: 2 High St Clifton
Tele No: BRISTOL 123456

There are several ways of storing files in memory. The first way is by storing the whole file in one array, file$(100,3). In the example above, file$(1,1) would contain 'A Aardvark', file$(1,2) would contain '2 High St Clifton' and file$(1,3) would contain 'BRISTOL 123456'. (Remember that an array dimensioned to 100, eg file$(100), actually has space for 101 elements, as it begins at element zero.)

Method 2 is similar, but uses three separate arrays, name$(100), address$(100) and teleno$(100). All the information about Mr Aardvark has the subscript 1. A problem could arise here if the order of any of the arrays was changed, eg by sorting.

Method 3 uses a string array of one dimension, file$(100). The information is stored this time in continuous strings, eg file$(1) is 'A Aardvark*2 High St Clifton%BRISTOL 123456'. The '*' and '%' symbols are used to separate the fields, and are chosen as characters that are unlikely to appear in a normal entry. The computer can search for these and will know that the characters after the '%' contain the telephone number.

Method 4 uses a simple string variable that expands to take in the entries. In this case, file$ = 'A Aardvark*2 High St Clifton%BRISTOL 123456&B Abbey*4 The Avenue%BRISTOL654321& . . .' etc. This is limited to a length of 255 characters.

You will find examples of the first three methods used here in different programs, although the most frequent method chosen is either method two or three.

Acorn machines are designed to use two filing systems, tape and disk.

Most people start with a cassette-based system and upgrade to disks at a later stage. Although disks are much faster and provide better ways of accessing information, it is a good idea to have a cassette player handy in case trouble arrives! This book was word-processed on a BBC computer, and I have been forced to rely on cassettes on a couple of occasions or risk losing pages of text.

The file-handling methods described here work equally well on disks or cassettes as they employ serial files, although naturally enough the access times are much faster with a disk drive.

To inform the computer in a program that you wish to write to an external file (ie record data on a tape or disk), you have to open a channel. This is achieved by the line

channel = OPENOUT (filename$)

where filename$ is the name you have given to this file.

You now use the command

PRINT# channel, data

where data is each record being stored.

When you have finished entering information, you have to close the channel with the line

CLOSE# channel

To load this information back in from the tape, you need to tell the computer to expect data from the cassette port. This is achieved by opening a channel again, but this time one coming in.

channel = OPENIN(filename$)

You can now read from the file by using

INPUT# channel, data

and close at the end as before with

CLOSE# channel

Here is a typical file transfer section from a program. There are two procedures, PROC_save and PROC_load.

PROC_save and PROC_load

```
1000 DEFPROC_save
1010 CLS
1020 PRINTTAB(14,1)"SAVING FILE"
1030 PRINTTAB(0,3)STRING$(40,"*")
1040 INPUTTAB(0,6)"ENTER A NAME- "file$
1050 x%=OPENOUT(file$)
1060 PRINT#x%,number
1070 FOR X = 1 TO number
1080    PRINT#x%,entry$(X)
1090    NEXT X
1100 CLOSE#x%
1110 ENDPROC
1120
1130 DEFPROC_load
1140 CLS
1150 PRINTTAB(14,1)"LOADING FILE"
1160 PRINTTAB(0,3)STRING$(40,"*")
1170 INPUTTAB(0,6)"ENTER NAME - "file$
1180 x%=OPENIN(file$)
1190 INPUT#x%,number
1200 FOR X = 1 TO number
1210    INPUT#x%,entry$(X)
1220    NEXT X
1230 CLOSE#x%
1240 flag=1
1250 ENDPROC
```

Sorting

There are many different routines for sorting information into order. These sort routines are well documented in other books, and will not be considered in any great detail here. The routine that is used in this book most frequently is called a binary search. To demonstrate the principle behind this, I shall consider a number-guessing game that is sometimes used to check problem-solving strategies in young children. This program has been taken from the Programming for Education series of books by Patrick Hall and myself, also published by Sunshine Books.

For this game, you need a blackboard, a piece of paper, or just your memory. It is the familiar one of 'I am thinking of a number — ask me any question about it you like, but I can only reply using yes or no.' Faced with this problem for the first time, a young child may be inclined to guess. If he or she realises that the number can be anything under (say) 1000, it is not long before it is appreciated that the task is difficult, and that some sort of logical strategy must be employed.

This sort of game is a useful activity as it improves mental skills including memory and visualisation of a sort of internal number line. It also helps develop logical questioning and inquiry strategies. You can probably see that the most logical strategy to follow is to approximately divide the answer by two.

A typical series of questions may go as follows:

Number is 242.

Is it larger than 500? No.
Is it larger than 250? No.
Is it larger than 125? Yes.
Is it larger than 190? Yes.
Is it larger than 230? Yes.
Is it larger than 240? Yes.
Is it larger than 245? No.
Is it larger than 243? No.
Is it larger than 241? Yes.
Is it 242? Yes.

Using this binary chopping method, it is always possible to reach the number without guessing in less than 10 attempts — 2 raised to the power of 10 is of course 1024.

Here is a short program that shows you the upper and lower guess limits.

Number

```
 10  REM ** Number Guesser **
 20  REM ** A.J.S.  1/4/83  **
 30  REM
 40  MODE1
 50  REPEAT
 60     CLS
 70     score = 0
 80     bottom = 0
 90     PRINT"I will think of a number";
        ". You must try"'"to guess it ";
        "in as few guesses as you can"
100     PRINT"Choose a top limit for ";
105     INPUT"your number "top
```

```
110     number = RND(top)
120     REPEAT
130       PRINT"The number lies between"
          ;bottom;" and ";top
140       score = score + 1
150       PRINT '"Enter guess no."
          ;" ";
160       INPUT guess
170       IF guess = number THEN
          PROCright
180       IF guess > number THEN top =
          guess
190       IF guess < number THEN bottom=
          guess
200       UNTIL guess = number
210     PRINT"Press space bar to go ";
        "again"
220     A$ = GET$
230     UNTIL FALSE
240 END
250
260 DEF PROCright
270 PRINT"You got it in ";score;
    " goes"
280 ENDPROC
```

Notes on the program

Lines 50–230 contain the REPEAT–UNTIL loop. This will repeat the program until the (ESCAPE) key is pressed.

The program has been trimmed down to the bare essentials and, as it is self-explanatory, there is no instruction page.

Variable 'score' contains the number of guesses so far; 'top' is the upper limit for the number; and 'bottom' is the lower limit.

Lines 120–200 contain the input REPEAT loop. This is only terminated when guess = number.

If guess = number, then **line 170** sends control to PROCright at **line 260**, which simply prints out the number of attempts.

All sorting routines operate by comparing the value of one element in an array with the others. It doesn't matter whether the array contains numbers or strings. Strings also have a value that is the same as the ASCII value of the characters (A = 65, etc). One important point to note here is that upper case letters have different values to lower case: if you ask a computer to put in order APPLE, banana, and ZEBRA, then the result would be APPLE, ZEBRA, banana, rather surprising if you didn't realise how computers operated. In order to avoid this problem, all the letters can be converted to upper case by a defined function, or you could request the user to use only upper case in the instructions.

This is how a defined function can convert lower case into upper case.

Defined Function Conversion

```
1000 REM **   EXAMPLE ENTRY ROUTINE   **
1010
1020 REPEAT
1030    INPUT A$
1040    A$ = FNCONV(A$)
1050    PRINT A$
1060    UNTIL FALSE
1070
1080 REM  **   DEFINED FUNCTION   **
1090
1100 DEFFNCONV(X$)
1110 LOCAL Z$,A,B,C
1120 Z$ = " "
1130 A=0:B=0:C=0
1140 FOR A = 1 TO LEN X$
1150    B = ASC(MID$(X$,A,1))
1160    C = B - 32
1170    IF B>96 AND B<123 THEN B=C
1180    Z$ = Z$+CHR$(B)
1190    NEXT A
1200 = Z$
```


The way binary chopping works in a procedure to insert an element in the correct place is to jump to the middle of the array and compare the element there with the chosen element. If the chosen element is more than the value at this point in the array, the search continues in the first half of the array, if less, then the second half is searched. The number of elements to be checked is successively halved until the correct position is found. This results in log 2 n comparisons, so you will sometimes see the routine referred to as a logarithmic search.

Here is a typical binary search procedure.

Binary Sort

```
1000 REM **   BINARY SORT DEMO   **
1010 REM
1020 REM **        AJS 2/4/83       **
1030
1040 DIMA$(30)
1050 MODE 1
1060
1070 PROC_makearray
1080 PROC_showarray(0,"ORIGINAL")
1090 PROC_sort(25)
1100 PRINTTAB(0,0);
1110 PROC_showarray(20,"SORTED")
1120 STOP
1130
1140 DEFPROC_makearray
1150
1160 REM  GENERATES AN ARRAY
1170 REM  OF 25 ELEMENTS
1180
1190 FOR N=1 TO 25
1200    A$(N)  = CHR$(RND(26)+64)+
       CHR$(RND(26)+64)
1210    NEXT N
1220 ENDPROC
1230
1240 DEFPROC_showarray(tab,title$)
1250 PRINTTAB(tab,1)title$
1260 FOR N=1 TO 25
1270    PRINTTAB(tab,N+2) A$(N)
1280    NEXT N
1290 ENDPROC
1300
1310 REM  **    SORT ROUTINE    **
1320
1330 REM   THIS WILL SORT AN ARRAY
1340 REM   OF number% ELEMENTS
1350 REM   A$(number%) IS THE ARRAY
1360 REM   A% and B% ARE LOOP
1370 REM   COUNTERS, C% HOLDS THE
1380 REM   BINARY DIVISION, D IS
1390 REM   A TEMPORARY COUNTER AND
1400 REM   E$ IS A TEMPORARY STORE
```

```
1410
1420 DEFPROC_sort(number%)
1430 LOCALA%,B%,C%,D%,E$
1440 C%=(number%) DIV 2
1450  REPEAT
1460   FOR B%=1+C% TO number%
1470     FOR A%=B%-C% TO 1 STEP -C%
1480       D%=A%+C%
1490       IF A$(A%)<=A$(D%) THEN 1540
1500       E$=A$(A%)
1510       A$(A%)=A$(D%)
1520       A$(D%)=E$
1530     NEXT A%
1540    NEXT B%
1550   C%=C% DIV2
1560   UNTIL C%=0
1570 ENDPROC
```

Notes on the program

The actual sort routine is held in PROC_sort. The first part of the program merely generates a random string array and prints the contents.

Line 1040 reserves space for up to 30 elements.

PROC_makearray chooses random upper case letters and loads them into array A$.

PROC_showarray has an example of parameter passing.

Lines 1080 and **1110** call PROC_showarray and also send information — the tab position for printing and the title — that is used inside that procedure.

PROC_sort also needs to have a parameter passed, in this case the number of elements to be sorted. **Line 1430** declares local variables that are to be used only in this procedure.

CHAPTER 2
The Domestic Servant

Annual expenditure and monthly analysis

Computers have been used for several years in offices, but only recently have they been cheap enough to consider for business purposes in the home. It is probably a good idea to look at the jobs that they could reasonably be expected to do before charging madly into program design.

Most people have a general idea of how much their cars cost them in terms of miles per gallon and how much oil is used, but they do not usually keep detailed records of miles travelled and true cost per month. A fall in mpg could warn you of trouble at an early stage, as could an increase in oil usage. If you keep records accurately, you are likely to get a shock — most people spend far more on owning a car than they realise!

The first program in this chapter is a car log that needs to be updated once a month. It shows you how much you spend on petrol, oil and other expenses, such as road tax, etc, and calculates mpg per month. Monthly averages as well the totals so far are available, and it is easy to add printer routines to obtain hard copy. If you travel a lot, then you could change it to cope with weekly input. As with most file programs, you will need to store this on one cassette, and keep another cassette for data. This is a sensible thing to do as the program itself contains no data — this is all stored on data files. If you use disks, then the same rule applies. If you are using cassettes, put the latest data on one side and, as you store fresh data, turn the tape over and use the other side. The reason for this is that, if for some unfortunate reason the tape is corrupted, you have still got last month's data at the other end of the cassette. If you use disks, you will no doubt already be in the habit of backing-up files in case of disaster.

Car Log is a rather long program to start with, but it demonstrates many of the techniques that are useful in long file-handling programs. If you find these are not required, they can be omitted. Notice the general structure of the program — PROC_intro is used to dimension the arrays used to store the monthly information.

The program is menu-driven: in other words, there is a screen of options that can be chosen. This is error-trapped in that the program will not allow you to choose to save data if there is none inside, and you cannot enter information unless all the values have been initialised. This is achieved by the use of two flags, 'flaginit' and 'flagenter', that are

```
            STATUS PAGE UP TO MONTH - 4
**********************************************
        TOTAL  MILAGE  =              3000.00
        TOTAL  PETROL  =               481.00 L
        TOTAL  PETROL  =               105.95 GALS
        TOTAL  PETROLMONEY  =          183.00
        TOTAL  OIL  =                    8.00 L
        TOTAL  OILMONEY  =              20.00
        TOTAL  EXTRAS  =               29.00


        PETROL CONSUMPTION

            =         6.24 MILES PER LITRE

        OR       28.32 MILES PER GALLON

        PETROL COST PER MILE=          0.06

        TOTAL COST/MILE       =        0.08

        TOTAL COST            =      232.00

        PRESS SPACE BAR TO CONTINUE
```

Figure 2.1: Screen Dump from Car Log.

initially zero, but are set to a value of one if certain conditions are met. They are called flags because they 'wave' a message if they are set.

It is usual to include instructions in the use of a program on a screen or in a printed guide. There is not enough room in the memory to provide detailed instructions, but the program has been made as clear as possible to avoid this necessity. Other particular features are mentioned in the notes.

Car Log

```
1000 REM   ***    CAR LOG     ***
1010 REM
1020 REM   ***   AJS 2/2/84   ***
1030
1040 MODE6
1050 PROC_intro
1060 PROC_colour
1070
1080 REPEAT
1090    PROC_menu
1100    UNTIL FALSE
1110
1120 DEFPROC_intro
```

```
1130 flagenter=0
1140 DIM milage(12)
1150 DIM petrol(12)
1160 DIM pmoney(12)
1170 DIM oil(12)
1180 DIM omoney(12)
1190 DIM extras(12)
1200 ENDPROC
1210
1220 DEFPROC_colour
1230 VDU19,0,4;0;
1240 VDU19,7,2;0;
1250 COLOUR 128
1260 ENDPROC
1270
1280 DEFPROC_menu
1290 CLS
1300 PRINTTAB(14,2)"CAR LOG"
1310 PRINTTAB(0,3)STRING$(40,"*")
1320 PRINTTAB(8,7)"OPTIONS:-"
1330 PRINTTAB(8,9)"1 INITIALISE FILE"
1340 PRINTTAB(8,11)
     "2 ENTER INFORMATION"
1350 PRINTTAB(8,13)"3 STATUS PAGE"
1360 PRINTTAB(8,15)"4 MONTHLY CHECK"
1370 PRINTTAB(8,17)"5 LOAD FILE"
1380 PRINTTAB(8,19)"6 SAVE FILE"
1390 PRINTTAB(8,21)"PRESS A NUMBER"
1400 REPEAT
1410    Z=GET
1420    UNTIL Z>48 AND Z<55
1430 IF Z = 49 THEN PROC_check
1440 IF Z = 50 THEN PROC_enter
1450 IF Z = 51 AND flagenter=1 THEN
     PROC_status
1460 IF Z = 52 AND flagenter=1 THEN
     PROC_monthly
1470 IF Z = 53 THEN PROC_load:
     flagenter=1
1480 IF Z = 54 AND flagenter=1 THEN
     PROC_save
1490 ENDPROC
1500
1510 DEFPROC_check
```

```
1520 CLS
1530 PRINTTAB(8,2)
     "ARE YOU SURE YOU WANT TO"
1540 PRINTTAB(8,4)
     "INITIALISE THE FILE?"
1550 REPEAT
1560    Z$=GET$
1570    UNTIL Z$="Y" OR Z$="N"
1580 IF Z$="Y" THEN PROC_init
1590 ENDPROC
1600
1610 DEFPROC_init
1620 REPEAT
1630    CLS
1640    month=0
1650    totalmilage=0
1660    totalpetrol=0
1670    totalpmoney=0
1680    totaloil=0
1690    totalomoney=0
1700    totalextras=0
1710    PRINTTAB(12,2)"INITIALISE FILE"
1720    PRINTTAB(0,3)STRING$(40,"*")
1730    INPUTTAB(2,4)
        "ENTER THE DATE (eg 25/04/83) "
        startdate$
1740    startmonthnum$=
        RIGHT$(startdate$,5)
1750    startmonth$=
        LEFT$(startmonthnum$,2)
1760    startmonth=VAL(startmonth$)
1770    INPUTTAB(2,6)
        "ENTER THE START MILAGE "
        startmilage
1780    PRINTTAB(2,20)"IS THIS CORRECT?"
1790    Z$=GET$
1800    UNTIL Z$="Y"
1810 ENDPROC
1820
1830 DEFPROC_enter
1840 REPEAT
1850    CLS
1860    PRINTTAB(12,2)"NEW INFORMATION"
1870    PRINTTAB(0,3)STRING$(40,"*")
```

```
1880    INPUTTAB(2,4)
        "ENTER THE DATE (eg 13/04/83) "
        date$
1890    date$=RIGHT$(date$,5)
1900    date$=LEFT$(date$,2)
1910    date=VAL(date$)+12
1920    UNTIL (date-startmonth+12) MOD12
        =month+1
1930 month=(date-startmonth+12) MOD 12
1940 PRINTTAB(4,6)"MONTH "month
1950 INPUTTAB(4,8)"ENTER NEW MILAGE "
     milage(month)
1960 totalmilage=milage(month)-
     startmilage
1970 INPUTTAB(4,10)
     "ENTER PETROL IN LITRES "
     petrol(month)
1980 totalpetrol=totalpetrol+
     petrol(month)
1990 INPUTTAB(4,12)
     "ENTER MONEY SPENT ON PETROL #"
     pmoney(month)
2000 totalpmoney=totalpmoney+
     pmoney(month)
2010 INPUTTAB(4,14)
     "ENTER OIL IN LITRES "oil(month)
2020 totaloil=totaloil+oil(month)
2030 INPUTTAB(4,16)
     "ENTER MONEY SPENT ON OIL #"
     omoney(month)
2040 totalomoney=totalomoney+
     omoney(month)
2050 INPUTTAB(4,18)
     "ENTER MONEY SPENT ON EXTRAS #"
     extras(month)
2060 totalextras=totalextras+
     extras(month)
2070 PRINTTAB(2,20)
     "PRESS SPACE BAR TO CONTINUE"
2080 REPEAT
2090    Z$ = GET$
2100    UNTIL Z$=" "
2110 flagenter=1
2120 ENDPROC
```

```
2130
2140 DEFPROC_monthly
2150 CLS
2160 PRINTTAB(12,2)"MONTHLY REPORT"
2170 PRINTTAB(0,3)STRING$(40,"*")
2180 PRINTTAB(4,4)
     "ENTER THE MONTH YOU WISH TO SEE"
2190 RESTORE
2200 PRINT
2210 FOR N = 1 TO 12
2220    READ mon$
2230    PRINTmon$
2240    NEXT N
2250 FOR N = 12-startmonth TO
        (12-startmonth)+11
2260    PRINT TAB(15,N+2)N MOD 12+1
2270    NEXT N
2280 REPEAT
2290    INPUT Z
2300    UNTIL Z>0 AND Z<13 AND Z<= month
2310 CLS
2320 @%=&20209
2330 milage(0)=startmilage
2340 PRINTTAB(12,2)"MONTH NUMBER - "
     STR$(Z)
2350 PRINTTAB(0,3)STRING$(40,"*")
2360 PRINTTAB(6,6)"MILAGE         - "
     milage(Z)-milage(Z-1)
2370 PRINTTAB(6,8)"PETROL         - "
     petrol(Z)" L"
2380 PRINTTAB(6,10)"PETROL MONEY - "
     pmoney(Z)
2390 PRINTTAB(6,12)"OIL            - "
     oil(Z)" L"
2400 PRINTTAB(6,14)"OIL MONEY      - "
     omoney(Z)
2410 PRINTTAB(6,16)"EXTRAS         - "
     extras(Z)
2420 consumption=0
2430 IF petrol(Z)>0 THEN
     consumption =
     (milage(Z)-milage(Z-1))/petrol(Z)
2440 PRINTTAB(6,18)"CONSUMPTION  - "
     consumption" MILES/L"
```

```
2450 PRINTTAB(6,20)"CONSUMPTION   - "
     consumption*4.54" MILES/GAL"
2460 @%=&10
2470 Z$=GET$
2480 ENDPROC
2490
2500 DEFPROC_status
2510 CLS
2520 PRINTTAB(6,2)
     "STATUS PAGE UP TO MONTH - ";month
2530 PRINTTAB(0,3)STRING$(40,"*")
2540 @%=&20209
2550 PRINTTAB(4,4)
     "TOTAL MILAGE =           "
     totalmilage
2560 PRINTTAB(4,5)
     "TOTAL PETROL =           "
     totalpetrol;" L"
2570 PRINTTAB(4,6)
     "TOTAL PETROL =           "
     totalpetrol/4.54;" GALS"
2580 PRINTTAB(4,7)
     "TOTAL PETROLMONEY =   "
     totalpmoney
2590 PRINTTAB(4,8)
     "TOTAL OIL =              "
     totaloil;" L"
2600 PRINTTAB(4,9)
     "TOTAL OILMONEY =     "totalomoney
2610 PRINTTAB(4,10)
     "TOTAL EXTRAS =       "totalextras
2620 PRINTTAB(4,13)"PETROL CONSUMPTION"
2630 consumption=
     totalmilage/totalpetrol
2640 PRINTTAB(4,15)
     " = "consumption" MILES PER LITRE"
2650 impcons=consumption*4.54
2660 PRINTTAB(4,17)
     "OR "impcons" MILES PER GALLON"
2670 total=totalpmoney+totalomoney+
     totalextras
2680 PRINTTAB(4,19)
     "PETROL COST PER MILE="
     totalpmoney/totalmilage
```

```
2690 PRINTTAB(4,21)
     "TOTAL COST/MILE      ="
     total/totalmilage
2700 PRINTTAB(4,23)
     "TOTAL COST            ="total
2710 @%=&10
2720 PRINTTAB(2,25)
     "PRESS SPACE BAR TO CONTINUE";
2730 REPEAT
2740   Z$=GET$
2750   UNTIL Z$=" "
2760 ENDPROC
2770
2780 DEFPROC_save
2790 CLS
2800 PRINTTAB(12,2)"SAVING FILE"
2810 PRINTTAB(0,3)STRING$(40,"*")
2820 INPUT ' "SAVING" '"ENTER A NAME- "
     file$
2830 x%=OPENOUT(file$)
2840 PRINT#x%,startmonth
2850 PRINT#x%,startmilage
2860 PRINT#x%,month
2870 PRINT#x%,totalmilage
2880 PRINT#x%,totalpetrol
2890 PRINT#x%,totalpmoney
2900 PRINT#x%,totaloil
2910 PRINT#x%,totalomoney
2920 PRINT#x%,totalextras
2930 FOR N=1TOmonth
2940   PRINT#x%,milage(N)
2950   PRINT#x%,petrol(N)
2960   PRINT#x%,pmoney(N)
2970   PRINT#x%,oil(N)
2980   PRINT#x%,omoney(N)
2990   PRINT#x%,extras(N)
3000   NEXT N
3010 CLOSE#x%
3020 CLS
3030 ENDPROC
3040
3050 DEFPROC_load
3060 CLS
3070 PRINTTAB(12,2)"LOADING FILE"
```

```
3080 PRINTTAB(0,3)STRING$(40,"*")
3090 INPUT '"LOADING" '"ENTER A NAME- "
     file$
3100  x%=OPENIN(file$)
3110 INPUT#x%,startmonth
3120 INPUT#x%,startmilage
3130 INPUT#x%,month
3140 INPUT#x%,totalmilage
3150 INPUT#x%,totalpetrol
3160 INPUT#x%,totalpmoney
3170 INPUT#x%,totaloil
3180 INPUT#x%,totalomoney
3190 INPUT#x%,totalextras
3200 FOR N=1TOmonth
3210     INPUT#x%,milage(N)
3220     INPUT#x%,petrol(N)
3230     INPUT#x%,pmoney(N)
3240     INPUT#x%,oil(N)
3250     INPUT#x%,omoney(N)
3260     INPUT#x%,extras(N)
3270     NEXT N
3280 CLOSE#x%
3290 CLS
3300 ENDPROC
3310
3320 DATA JANUARY,FEBRUARY,MARCH,APRIL
3330 DATA MAY,JUNE,JULY,AUGUST
3340 DATA SEPTEMBER,OCTOBER,NOVEMBER
3350 DATA DECEMBER
```

Notes on the program

Line 1040 puts the program into mode 6. The program would originally run in mode 1, but reformatting the lines has increased the size.

PROC_intro initialises flags and reserves space for the arrays that will hold the monthly information. The program will hold information for one year, but it is designed to cope with entries that start in any month.

PROC_colour sets the printing colour to green, and the background colour to blue.

PROC_menu contains the main menu to which control returns.

Line 1310 prints a line of asterisks across the screen.

Lines 1400–1420 ensure that only suitable number keys are read from the keyboard.

Lines 1430–1480 send control to various procedures. Variable 'flagenter' is set to 0 initially, and to a value of 1 once information has been entered. This is to prevent the program attempting to save non-existent files.

PROC_check makes sure that you wish to initialise the record before it enters the next procedure.

PROC_init allows the user to set the start month, and the mileage shown in the car at the beginning.

Lines 1620–1800 contain a REPEAT loop, so that if any of the entered data is incorrect, it can be altered.

PROC_enter accepts input each month. This has to be for the following month, or the input is not accepted. If there are no entries for one particular month you will have to enter zero for all entries. This is to prevent 'division by zero' errors and other spurious happenings.

Line 1920 uses the MOD function to give the month a number: n MOD 12 gives the remainder when n is divided by 12, eg:

$$15 \text{ MOD } 12 = 3$$

The function DIV produces the number of times n can be divided by 12.

$$15 \text{ DIV } 12 = 1$$

Lines 1950–2060 accept the input of all the necessary information.

Line 2110 sets the variable 'flagenter' to show that there is data in the arrays.

PROC_monthly is in two sections.

The first runs from **lines 2170–2300** and selects the month to be examined. **Line 2190** sends the data pointer to the first data line. **Lines 2250** and **2260** look rather complicated, but they simply format the months neatly and position the months opposite the correct month numbers. **Line 2300** makes sure that the user cannot look at a month that does not yet have any information.

The second section runs from **lines 2310–2480**, and prints the details of the month that has been selected.

Line 2320 sets the format of all numbers to two decimal places. This is to avoid results such as:

Miles per gallon = 24.672358

Lines 2340–2450 show the contents of the particular arrays. The program asks for petrol to be input in litres, rather than gallons, as pumps with the display in gallons seem to have disappeared. If you live somewhere with antiquated garages, you can alter the input routine.

Line 2460 sets the number printing format back to normal.

PROC_status gives the user a breakdown of how much has been spent in different areas up to the most recent entry. It also shows the average petrol consumption, cost per mile, and totals of all arrays.

PROC_save and **PROC_load** seem larger than most save and load procedures in this book. This is only because a lot of different information has to be entered, and this saves a certain amount of calculation.

Lines 3320–3350 contain the data for PROC_monthly.

Storing and sorting data

Computers are very efficient at storing and sorting data. In the world at large, this has resulted in programs that hold information on a wide variety of subjects. These databases can be interrogated and relevant information extracted. Some present examples of this are the vehicle licence centre in Swansea, many library records, Ceefax, Oracle and Prestel. Some of these, like the licence centre, are closed to the general public, while others, like the two teletext systems, are totally public — all that is necessary is suitable receiving equipment.

Teletext and viewdata systems appear similar, as each page of information is formed in the same way from 25 lines of 40 characters using the same block graphics. In fact there are far greater differences than similarities. Teletext broadcasts its data on the spare lines at the top of a TV picture. This data is held in the form of pages of text that each have a number. This means that it is all one-way — you can't transmit back up the TV carrier wave. To extract information, you need to find an index page. Once you have found the page number from this, you can go directly to the relevant screen.

Viewdata systems, like Prestel, are accessed differently: instead of transmitting all the pages one after the other every few seconds, the user selects which page needs to be sent down the telephone line. As the number of pages is far larger than teletext, index pages are not usually used. Instead, each page leads to several others in a tree structure. The choice of exits is presented in the form of a menu, and users choose their own routes. If you know the number of a certain page, it is possible to go straight there and the system is, naturally enough, two-way, allowing you to send data back to the host computer. It cannot, however, perform calculations for you, and is primarily an example of computerised communication.

The licence centre at Swansea and most business databases do not hold their information in the form of pages. The information is still often selected from menus, but the displays are different each time, and pages would be an uneconomical way to store so many alternatives.

Simple databases are easy to set up on home computers, and these can mimic the features found on large mainframe computers. Before setting up a database, it is a good idea to ask a few questions about the usefulness of such a system. One program you may often see in books and magazines is a computerised telephone book. While it may teach you a little about sorting and selecting information on a computer, it is not really a practical program. All the names and addresses of your friends and contacts are stored on a file; you enter their name or part of the address and out comes the number in less than a second.

If you have a very large number of friends, and your computer is permanently set up next to the phone with the relevant program installed, then this could be a quick system. But in most cases, setting up the computer, finding the correct cassette and waiting for it to load would take at least five minutes. In this time you could have turned to the telephone section in your diary, made the call and by now be sitting down with a cup of tea! As this book is supposed to contain useful programs, I have left out a phone/number address book listing, and moved towards a general information-handling program that can be adapted to different requirements.

If you have a small business with several hundred customers, and want to computerise some of your information, then I would suggest that a program that lets you ask detailed questions would be more useful than a simple phone list. I am a great believer in using pencil and paper if it's quicker than the computer.

If you have an Electron that came in all the pretty packaging, then you may have been intrigued by one of the pictures on the outside showing a woman in a kitchen with her computer sitting on the work-top. It's possible that she's a busy housewife catching up on her Open University studies as she prepares dinner, but I imagine that Acorn Computers would prefer us to think that she's using it to actually help with the cooking.

Simply using a computer to store recipes would be no quicker than using a book. A useful program would use the power of a computer to sort, cross-reference data, and even carry out calculations for you. To begin with, a list of requirements could be drawn up. The program should:

a) Allow you to choose suitable dishes for each stage of the meal.
b) Show you the recipe and the cooking time.
c) Help you calculate quantities according to the number of guests.
d) Convert from imperial to metric units and vice versa.
e) Calculate the cooking time according to the weight of the food.
f) Calculate who should do the washing up.

All of these are fairly easy to arrange, with the possible exception of the last! If you are wondering at this stage what has happened to your information retrieval program which will give you a home database to rival Prestel or the Source, then this trip into the kitchen is being used as an example. As with all the programs in this book, it is hoped that you will modify it to your own requirements.

Chef is menu-driven (no pun intended) and gives you the choice of entering fresh recipes, selecting food from those already present, converting weights and measures, and calculating cooking times according to two different methods.

The cooking times and conversion sections are fairly straightforward and demonstrate two different ways of storing variables. Cooking time factors for different meats are held as variables in program lines, whereas the conversion factors are held in data lines and read in as necessary.

The way the particular recipes are stored is not quite so obvious. When you enter recipes, you are asked to give the dish a title and a series of codes, eg if the recipe is Spaghetti Bolognese, it's beef, pasta, spicy and is usually served hot, so you would enter 6, then 9, then 10 and finally 13. (The codes are explained clearly in the program.) The computer now works out a single code for this particular combination by using a binary translation routine. This sounds complicated, but it is really quite simple. There are 15 code numbers, and these represent the powers of two that will be added together. The example above is coded as follows:

$$6 \text{ is coded as } 2\,^\wedge\, 6 \text{ or } \quad 64$$
$$9 \text{ is coded as } 2\,^\wedge\, 9 \text{ or } \quad 512$$
$$10 \text{ is coded as } 2\,^\wedge\, 10 \text{ or } 1024$$
$$13 \text{ is coded as } 2\,^\wedge\, 13 \text{ or } 8192$$

$$\text{Total} \quad 9792$$

The final code for the dish is the sum of these codes, ie 9792.

Expressed as a 16-digit binary number, this would be 0010011001000000. If you realise that a 1 means the attribute is present, and a 0 means it is absent, then you can see that this code number doesn't have attributes 0 to 5 (starting from the right), but does have a 1 for digits 6, 9, 10 and 13, so these attributes are present. There are a total of 65,535 different combinations of codes possible, although some of them are clearly most unlikely. (Can you imagine a dish that is both a soup and a sweet, contains beef and fish, and can be eaten hot or cold?)

If you were to adapt the program to store information about people, however, then the categories could stand for the presence or absence of blue eyes, dark hair, a beard, owns a house, owns a car, etc, and then all 64K of possibilities might be necessary.

The reason why this form of coding is useful is that it is very easy to ask the computer to check whether the different bits of a number are set or not, ie are 0 or 1. When you search for a dish to cook one evening, the program asks you to enter the code to search for. For instance, if you entered 9, then all the pasta meals would be selected. If you chose 9 and 6, then only those pasta meals with beef would appear. The computer achieves the selection as follows.

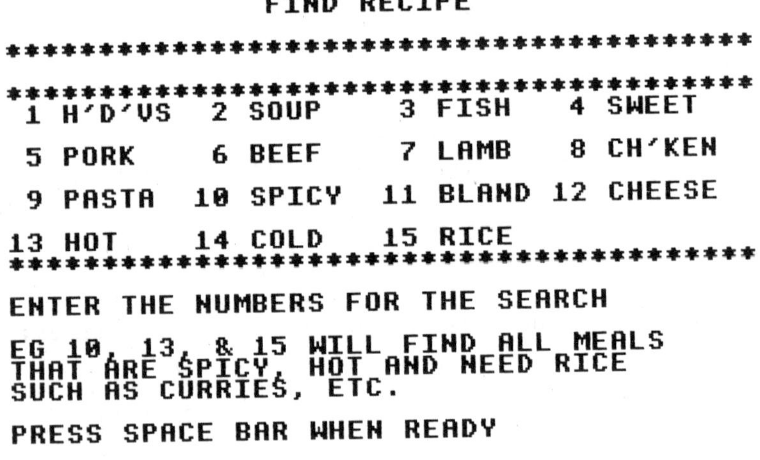

Figure 2.2: Screen Dump from Chef.

Most copies of BASIC have as well as arithmetic operators others called logical operators. These are AND, OR, NOT, etc. It is fairly easy to see how they work when used to compare the truth of statements, eg

IF A>B OR A<C THEN . . . ACTION

will result in the action taking place if either of the two conditions are true.

IF A>B AND A<C THEN . . . ACTION

will result in the action taking place only if both of the two conditions are true.

If logical operators are used to compare two numbers, then some strange results are produced.

PRINT 14 AND 20

will produce the answer 4. This is because the actual bits of the binary equivalent are compared.

14 is   00001110 in binary form
20 is   00010100 in binary form
               ----
14 AND 20 is 00000100

Notice that both the top and bottom rows have to have a one to produce a one in the answer. Two zeros or a zero and a one merely result in a zero in the answer.

PRINT 14 OR 20

will produce the answer 30. Again, the bits are compared individually.

14 is   00001110
20 is   00010100
               ----
14 OR 20   00011110

Notice that, this time, the OR operator produces a one in the answer line if either or both of the two rows have a one. The only time a zero is produced in the answer line is when both rows have a zero. Because of this, OR can be considered to be the reverse of AND.

In the recipe program, the effect of AND is used to test if particular bits are set. If you want to select all those dishes that contain lamb, then their codes will contain 2^7 or 128. All the codes are tested to see if the seventh bit is set by ANDing the codes with 2^7. Those that have the seventh bit set will produce the answer 2^7.

At first sight logical operators appear most illogical, but if you try out some examples for yourself, and work out what is happening at the bit level, you will find you have acquired a better knowledge of how computers work.

Chef

```
1000 REM   ** CHEF DE CUISINE **
1010 REM
1020 REM   **   AJS 10/10/83    **
1030
1040 MODE6
1050 PROC_init
1060 REPEAT
1070    PROC_menu
1080    UNTIL FALSE
1090
1100 DEFPROC_init
1110 DIMdishname$(20)
1120 DIMcode%(20)
1130 DIMingred$(20)
1140 VDU19,0,6;0;
1150 VDU19,7,4;0;
1160 flag = 0
1170 FORN=1TO20
1180    ingred$(N)=STRING$(255,"*")
1190    ingred$(N)=""
1200    NEXT N
1210 dishno=0
1220 ENDPROC
1230
1240 DEFPROC_menu
1250 CLS
1260 PRINTTAB(12,1)"CHEF DE CUISINE"
1270 PRINTTAB(0,3)STRING$(40,"*")
1280 PRINTTAB(4,6)"1 ENTER NEW RECIPE"
1290 PRINTTAB(4,8)"2 SELECT MEAL"
1300 PRINTTAB(4,10)"3 COOKING MEAT"
1310 PRINTTAB(4,12)"4 METRIC C/VERSION"
1320 PRINTTAB(4,14)"5 SAVE FILE"
1330 PRINTTAB(4,16)"6 LOAD FILE"
1340 PRINTTAB(4,18)"7 STOP PROGRAM"
1350 PRINTTAB(4,20)"CHOOSE A NUMBER"
1360 REPEAT
1370    Z$ = GET$
1380    Z=VAL(Z$)
1390    UNTIL Z>0 AND Z<8
1400 IF Z=1 THEN PROC_enter
1410 IF Z=2 AND flag=1 THEN PROC_select
```

```
1420 IF Z=3 THEN PROC_meat
1430 IF Z=4 THEN PROC_convert
1440 IF Z=5 AND flag=1 THEN PROC_save
1450 IF Z=6 THEN PROC_load:flag=1
1460 IF Z=7 THEN STOP
1470 ENDPROC
1480
1490 DEFPROC_enter
1500 CLS
1510 PRINTTAB(11,1)"ENTER NEW RECIPE"
1520 PRINTTAB(0,3)STRING$(40,"*")
1530 PRINTTAB(2,5)
     "YOU WILL BE ASKED SOME QUESTIONS"
1540 PRINTTAB(3,7)
     "SO THE FOOD CAN BE CLASSIFIED"
1550 PRINTTAB(10,9)"WHEN YOU ARE READY"
1560 PRINTTAB(12,11)"PRESS [RETURN]"
1570 PRINTTAB(9,13)"OR PRESS SPACE BAR"
1580 PRINTTAB(7,15)
     "TO RETURN TO MAIN MENU"
1590 REPEAT
1600    Z = GET
1610    UNTIL Z = 32 OR Z = 13
1620 IF Z = 32 THEN ENDPROC ELSE CLS
1630 dishno=dishno+1
1640 PRINTTAB(11,1)"ENTER NEW RECIPE"
1650 PRINTTAB(0,3)STRING$(40,"*")
1660 PRINTTAB(4,4)
     "ENTER THE NAME OF DISH NO. ";
     dishno
1670 INPUTTAB(5,6)dishname$(dishno)
1680 PRINTTAB(4,8)
     "LOOK AT THE FOLLOWING CHART"
1690 VDU28,0,24,39,9
1700 PROC_foodcodes
1710 VDU26
1720 COLOUR128
1730 PRINT
1740 VDU28,0,24,39,18
1750 PRINTTAB(0,26)
     "ENTER THE NUMBERS TO CODE ";
     "YOUR DISH."
1760 PRINT
1770 PRINT"EG BEEF CURRY IS MEAT, ";
```

```
         "BEEF, SPICY AND"
1780 PRINT"HOT AND NEEDS RICE, ";
         "SO THE CODES ARE"
1790 PRINTTAB(12)"6, 10, 13, & 15"
1800 PRINT
1810 PRINT"PRESS SPACE BAR WHEN READY";
1820 Z$=GET$
1830 REPEAT
1840    totalcode=0
1850    CLS
1860    PRINT"ENTER THE NUMBERS ";
           "ONE AT A TIME"
1870    PRINT"ENTER 'Z' TO STOP"
1880    REPEAT
1890      INPUT code$
1900      fdcode=VAL(code$)
1910      totalcode=totalcode+2^fdcode
1920      UNTIL code$="Z"
1930    PRINT"IS THIS CORRECT?"
1940    Z$ = GET$
1950    UNTIL Z$ = "Y"
1960 code%(dishno)=totalcode-1
1970 VDU26
1980 PROC_recipe
1990 ENDPROC
2000
2010 DEFPROC_recipe
2020 CLS
2030 PRINTTAB(12,1)"RECIPE DETAILS"
2040 PRINTTAB(0,3)STRING$(40,"*")
2050 PRINTTAB(1,5)"ENTER THE RECIPE ";
         "ONE LINE AT A TIME"
2060 PRINTTAB(1)"(NO PUNCTUATION)"
2070 PRINTTAB(1)
         "ENTER 'ZZZ' WHEN FINISHED"
2080 REPEAT
2090    INPUTentry$
2100    toolong=LEN(entry$)+
         LEN(ingred$(dishno))
2110    IF toolong>251 THEN
         ingred$(dishno)=ingred$(dishno)+
         "#":dishno=dishno+1
2120    ingred$(dishno) =
         ingred$(dishno)+"*"+entry$
```

```
2130    UNTIL entry$ = "ZZZ"
2140 len=LEN(ingred$(dishno))
2150 flag=1
2160 ingred$(dishno) =
     LEFT$(ingred$(dishno),len-4)
2170 ENDPROC
2180
2190 DEFPROC_select
2200 CLS
2210 PRINTTAB(14,1)"FIND RECIPE"
2220 PRINTTAB(0,3)STRING$(40,"*")
2230 PROC_foodcodes
2240 VDU26
2250 VDU28,0,24,39,15
2260 PRINTTAB(0,26)
     "ENTER THE NUMBERS FOR THE SEARCH"
2270 PRINT
2280 PRINT"EG 10, 13, & 15 ";
     "WILL FIND ALL MEALS"
2290 PRINT"THAT ARE SPICY, ";
     "HOT AND NEED RICE"
2300 PRINT"SUCH AS CURRIES, ETC."
2310 PRINT
2320 PRINT"PRESS SPACE BAR WHEN READY";
2330 Z$=GET$
2340 REPEAT
2350    totalchoice%=0
2360    CLS
2370    PRINT"ENTER THE CODES ";
     "'Z' TO STOP"
2380    REPEAT
2390      INPUT choicecode$
2400      chcode=VAL(choicecode$)
2410      totalchoice%=totalchoice%+
     2^chcode
2420      UNTIL choicecode$="Z"
2430    PRINT"IS THIS CORRECT?"
2440    Z$=GET$
2450    UNTIL Z$="Y"
2460 totalchoice%=totalchoice%-1
2470 VDU26
2480 CLS
2490 PROC_choose
2500 ENDPROC
```

```
2510
2520 DEFPROC_foodcodes
2530 PRINTSTRING$(40,"*");
2540 PRINT" 1 H'D'VS  2 SOUP      3 ";
     "FISH   4 SWEET"
2550 PRINT
2560 PRINT" 5 PORK      6 BEEF     7 ";
     "LAMB    8 CH'KEN"
2570 PRINT
2580 PRINT" 9 PASTA  10 SPICY   11 ";
     "BLAND 12 CHEESE"
2590 PRINT
2600 PRINT"13 HOT     14 COLD    15 ";
     "RICE"
2610 PRINTSTRING$(40,"*");
2620 VDU26
2630 ENDPROC
2640
2650 DEFPROC_choose
2660 FOR N=1 TO 20
2670    choice=0
2680    test%=totalchoice% AND code%(N)
2690    IF totalchoice% = test% THEN
        choice=1
2700    IF choice=1 THEN PRINT
        dishname$(N)
2710    IF choice=1 THEN PRINT
        "DO YOU WANT TO SEE THE RECIPE?"
2720    IF choice=1 THEN Z$=GET$
2730    IF choice=1 AND Z$="Y" THEN CLS:
        PROC_showrecipe
2740    NEXTN
2750 ENDPROC
2760
2770 DEFPROC_showrecipe
2780 PRINTTAB(5,1)dishname$(N)
2790 PRINTTAB(0,2)STRING$(40,"*");
2800 FORX=1TOLEN(ingred$(N))
2810    L$=MID$(ingred$(N),X,1)
2820    IF L$<>"*" AND L$<>"#" THEN
        PRINT L$;
2830    IF L$ = "*" THEN PRINT
2840    NEXT X
2850 IF L$="#" THEN N=N+1:GOTO 2800
```

```
2860 PRINT:PRINT
2870 PRINT"PRESS SPACE BAR TO CONTINUE"
2880 Z$=GET$
2890 CLS
2900 ENDPROC
2910
2920 DEFPROC_meat
2930 CLS
2940 PRINTTAB(12,1)"ROASTING GUIDE"
2950 PRINTTAB(0,3)STRING$(40,"*")
2960 PRINTTAB(10,5)"1 BEEF/MUTTON"
2970 PRINTTAB(10,7)"2 LAMB"
2980 PRINTTAB(10,9)"3 PORK"
2990 PRINTTAB(10,11)"4 VEAL/VENISON"
3000 PRINTTAB(10,13)"5 CHICKEN/RABBIT"
3010 PRINTTAB(10,15)"6 GROUSE/PHEASANT"
3020 PRINTTAB(10,17)"7 GOOSE/HARE"
3030 PRINTTAB(10,19)"8 TURKEY"
3040 PRINTTAB(10,21)"CHOOSE A NUMBER"
3050 Z=0
3060 REPEAT
3070    Z$ = GET$
3080    Z = VAL(Z$)
3090    UNTIL Z>0 AND Z<9
3100 IF Z=1 THEN time = 25
3110 IF Z=2 THEN time = 30
3120 IF Z=3 THEN time = 35
3130 IF Z=4 THEN time = 40
3140 IF Z=5 THEN time = 20
3150 IF Z=6 THEN time = 20
3160 IF Z=7 THEN time = 20
3170 IF Z=8 THEN time = 15
3180 PRINTTAB(10,23)"POUNDS OR GRAMS?"
3190 REPEAT
3200    Z$ = GET$
3210    UNTIL Z$ = "P" OR Z$ = "G"
3220 factor = 1
3230 IF Z$ = "G" THEN factor = 454
3240 INPUTTAB(10,25)"ENTER WEIGHT "wt
3250 CLS
3260 PRINTTAB(12,1)"ROASTING GUIDE"
3270 PRINTTAB(0,3)STRING$(40,"*")
3280 PRINTTAB(4,4)"METHOD ONE"
3290 PRINTTAB(4,6)
```

```
          "PREHEAT OVEN TO 475F/250C/MK9"
3300 PRINTTAB(4,8)
          "COOK MEAT FOR 15 mins OR UNTIL ";
          "BROWN"
3310 PRINTTAB(4,10)
          "REDUCE HEAT TO 350F/175C/MK4"
3320 min = INT(wt*time/factor)
3330 PRINTTAB(4,12)
          "ROAST FOR ";min;" MINUTES"
3340 PRINTTAB(0,13)STRING$(40,"*")
3350 PRINTTAB(4,14)"METHOD TWO"
3360 PRINTTAB(4,16)
          "PREHEAT OVEN TO 325F/150C/MK3"
3370 min=INT(min*1.5)
3380 PRINTTAB(4,18)"COOK MEAT FOR ";
          min;" MINUTES"
3390 PRINTTAB(4,20)"TURN UP HEAT FOR ";
          "LAST FEW MINUTES"
3400 PRINTTAB(4,22)"TO BROWN MEAT ";
          "AND ANY POTATOES"
3410 PRINTTAB(4,24)"PRESS SPACE BAR ";
          "TO CONTINUE";
3420 Z$ = GET$
3430 Z=0
3440 ENDPROC
3450
3460 DEFPROC_convert
3470 CLS
3480 PRINTTAB(12,1)"CONVERSIONS"
3490 PRINTTAB(0,3)STRING$(40,"*")
3500 PRINTTAB(2,4)"1 POUNDS TO GRAMS"
3510 PRINTTAB(2,6)"2 GRAMS TO POUNDS"
3520 PRINTTAB(2,8)"3 FL OZ TO ML"
3530 PRINTTAB(2,10)"4 ML TO FL OZ"
3540 PRINTTAB(2,12)"5 PTS TO L"
3550 PRINTTAB(2,14)"6 L TO PTS"
3560 PRINTTAB(2,16)"7 OZ TO G"
3570 PRINTTAB(2,18)"8 G TO OZ"
3580 PRINTTAB(2,20)"CHOOSE A NUMBER";
3590 Z=0
3600 REPEAT
3610   Z$ = GET$
3620   Z=VAL(Z$)
3630   UNTIL Z>0 AND Z<9
```

```
3640 PRINTTAB(20,20)"NUMBER ";Z;
     " CHOSEN"
3650 RESTORE
3660 FOR N = 1 TO Z
3670    READ factor
3680    NEXT N
3690 INPUTTAB(2,21)
     "ENTER VALUE FOR CONVERSION - "
     value
3700 @%=&20209
3710 PRINTTAB(2,22)"RESULT = ";
     value*factor
3720 @%=&10
3730 PRINTTAB(2,24)
     "PRESS SPACE BAR TO CONTINUE";
3740 Z$ = GET$
3750 Z=0
3760 ENDPROC
3770
3780 DEFPROC_load
3790 CLS
3800 PRINTTAB(12,1)"LOADING DATAFILE"
3810 PRINTTAB(0,3)STRING$(40,"*")
3820 INPUT ' "LOADING" '"ENTER A NAME-"
     file$
3830 x%=OPENIN(file$)
3840 INPUT#x%,dishno
3850 FOR N=1TOdishno
3860    INPUT#x%,dishname$(N)
3870    INPUT#x%,code%(N)
3880    INPUT#x%,ingred$(N)
3890    NEXT N
3900 CLOSE#x%
3910 ENDPROC
3920
3930 DEFPROC_save
3940 CLS
3950 PRINTTAB(12,1)"SAVING DATAFILE"
3960 PRINTTAB(0,3)STRING$(40,"*")
3970 INPUT ' "SAVING" ' "ENTER A NAME-"
     file$
3980 x%=OPENOUT(file$)
3990 PRINT#x%,dishno
4000 FOR N=1TOdishno
```

```
4010    PRINT#x%,dishname$(N)
4020    PRINT#x%,code%(N)
4030    PRINT#x%,ingred$(N)
4040    NEXT N
4050 CLOSE#x%
4060 ENDPROC
4070
4080 REM   ** conversion factor data **
4090 DATA 454, 0.0022, 28.4, 0.0352
4100 DATA 0.568, 1.76, 28.35, 0.0353
```

Notes on the program

PROC_init reserves space for the arrays and sets the background and foreground colours. The arrays are only dimensioned for 20 recipes but, as the program is in mode 6, there is probably room for more. If you do encounter the dreaded 'No room' message, you could use separate datafiles for different courses.

PROC_menu contains the list of alternatives and branches the program according to the keypress Z$. The variable 'flag' is used to check if there is any data in the program, and is set to a value of 1 if that is the case.

PROC_enter accepts new recipes.

Line 1690 defines a text window, so that the top of the display remains intact, while the bottom half can be cleared and scrolled according to the information being presented.

Lines 1680–1800 give instructions on how to select codes for the meal type selected.

Lines 1880–1920 accept the food codes as entered, and add them to the total code after converting them to the binary form explained earlier.

Line 1960 sets the code for that particular recipe to 'totalcode − 1'. This has to be done due to the fact that the last code entered is a 'Z', and **line 1910** adds this to the total. As letters have the value 0, and as 2 to the power of 0 is 1, this returns the correct value of the code without the value of the 'Z'.

Line 1970 sets the screen windows back to their original size.

PROC_recipe accepts the details of the recipe. **Line 2060** warns against using punctuation in the recipe. This is because commas act as string terminators; in other words the computer will ignore everything after a comma in a string input.

Recipes are entered into the array ingred$(n). Each time the

<RETURN> key is pressed, the line is added to the recipe$, together with an asterisk. If the string gets too long, ie in this case over 251 characters, the rest of the menu is entered into the next element of the array, and a hash character (#) is added to the end of the first section. When the recipe is being printed, the program will look for asterisks to tell it to generate a line feed, and the hash sign will send it to the next element of the array for the continuation. Without this ploy, recipes would be limited to about six lines.

Line 2150 sets the variable 'flag' to 1 to show that there is now data in the program.

PROC_select uses a reverse system to PROC_enter to find recipes with the correct codes. There are instructions included in **lines 2260–2320**.

Lines 2380–2420 turn the selected codes into the binary form, and the program is sent to PROC_choose to find any recipes that meet the specification.

PROC_foodcodes contains the food codes. These can be altered as you wish. You will need to enter the lines carefully in order to get neat formatting on the screen.

PROC_choose actually selects recipes in one line. **Line 2680** performs logical ANDing as explained earlier. If the choice of codes is present in any recipe, the user has the opportunity of ignoring the recipe, or of seeing it displayed on the screen.

PROC_showrecipe prints the contents of the chosen array elements on the screen, and uses the asterisks and hash characters to format the strings in the same form as they were initially entered.

Line 2850 contains a GOTO, so apologies are due to confirmed structuralists who may be reading this. I could have used another procedure but this would have been even more complex. If BBC BASIC had WHILE–ENDWHILE, this would not have proved necessary. The purpose of the GOTO is to send control to the start of the loop again if the recipe is stored in more than one element of the array.

PROC_meat provides another menu for various meat cooking times. **Lines 2940–3040** display the options. **Lines 3050–3170** take the chosen option and select a value for 'time'. This is in fact the cooking time per pound in minutes, so if you disagree with the values, they are easy to change.

Lines 3180–3250 ask for a weight in pounds or grams, and variable 'factor' is used to convert metric values into imperial. **Lines 3240–3410** print two standard cooking methods on the screen.

PROC_convert is also menu-driven and is used to perform a variety of conversions that may be useful in the kitchen. The conversion factors are held in data statements at the end of the program, and these are read in **line 3670** according to the requested option.

Line 3700 sets the number-printing format to two places of decimals and **line 3720** returns it to normal.

PROC_load and **PROC_save** are standard save and load routines and are used to save and load the number of dishes, their names, codes and the recipes.

Disclaimer: Neither the author nor the publishers can accept any responsibility for strange meals produced as a result of using this program!

Word-processing

Word-processors seem to be viewed by those in business as a godsend, and by the rest of the population as an unnecessary evil. Few weeks go by when we fail to suffer the intrusions of a few well-known companies on whose mailing lists we happen to appear: 'Congratulations, Mr X, you have been specially selected to receive six winning numbers in our prize draw. Won't the other inhabitants of Ytown be surprised when they see a new Porsche 928 standing outside of No 1, Z Avenue . . . ?'

The use of word-processors in producing standard letters is well-known, and they undoubtedly save a lot of work in a busy office. Originally designed to store text for day-to-day use, they are now capable of many refinements and advanced techniques. The most recent models which can not only format text but also typeset newsprint have caused several problems in Fleet St., as yet another skilled trade becomes automated.

The most important feature of computers is their adaptability, ie the fact that they are not designed specifically for any one purpose, so it is possible to emulate many of the features of a professional dedicated word-processor on an Electron or BBC micro, although it is hoped that you will want to put it to better use than the example used at the beginning of this section!

When designing a program like this, it is a good idea to make a list of the features that are desirable, and then to see which of these can be incorporated in the software. Here are some of the features that could be available:

a) Saving and reloading of text.
b) Text editing.
c) Formatting of text on screen.

d) Sending text to a printer.
e) Sending printer codes.
f) Text justification.
g) Automatic word-wrap.
h) Search and replace.
i) Word count.
j) Memory free.

The first thing to decide is how the text is going to be stored in the computer. Some word-processors reserve a section of memory in which the characters are stored as they are entered, and a pointer is used to indicate where text is to be inserted. This method is possible on the Electron and BBC machines, but is rather complicated to arrange and even more difficult to explain. The method chosen here follows on from methods used to store information in other programs in this book, that is to use an array A\$, with 100 elements. Each element is capable of storing well over 200 characters but, in this program, each element will only be required to store one line, so it is unlikely to have to hold more than 80 characters.

The program is menu-driven, and the first option is to change the format of the text about to be entered. Values are assigned in PROC_init at the start of the program that allow for 55 characters per line, a left margin 12 characters in and a total number of 66 lines per page. The lines are one apart, ie there are no spaces between lines. As the line length affects the way the text is stored, changing this parameter cannot alter text already entered, although you can change subsequent line length at any time during execution of the program. Altering the left margin and line spacing parameters will change the format of the whole document at any time.

In text entry mode, GET\$ is used to check the keyboard and each key pressed is added to the array element, which starts off as an empty string. As it lengthens, it eventually reaches the length set by the line length parameter in the formatting module. The program waits for the next space character or <RETURN> press, then strips off the whole of the last word and attaches it to the beginning of the next element of the array, which means that there are no words that start in one line and continue in the next. This is termed 'auto word-wrap'.

To escape from entry mode, you can choose any character that is not likely to be used as text, or you could use a control character. In the listing I have used the hash character, '#', as it is unlikely to occur in normal text situations. If this is pressed, control jumps back to the menu module and you can choose to look at the formatted text. This option shows the text as it would appear in its final form, complete with correct margin, line spacing and line length. Down the lefthand edge of the screen appear the line numbers: these are important, as you need some sort of reference to edit lines. You are instructed to press the space bar at the end of the document to return to the menu. If you now select to enter text again, you will find yourself at the start of the next line. If you want to continue exactly from the point you have reached, you will have to select 'edit text' from the menu and enter the whole line again.

The majority of the variables used in this program are suffixed by a '%' character, denoting the fact that they are integer variables. Apart from taking up less space in memory, you should notice a decrease in processing time when integer variables are used.

If you do not have a printer or access to one, this program is of limited use, although it does produce text files stored in standard ASCII format that could be printed out from any BBC or Electron computer equipped with a printer interface. A small warning is needed at this point: the way that Acorn machines store files means that each line of text is stored back to front. If you have disks, write some text using the program, save it under the file name 'text', and then look at the file by entering '*DUMP text' (no quotes necessary). A hexadecimal dump appears on the screen of the file, along with the text — all backwards!

```
0000    40   00   00   00   13   00   32   0D   @.....2.
0008    65   76   6F   72   47   20   6D   75   evorG mu
```

If you wanted to make your files compatible with professional ROM-based word-processors like View or Wordwise, you will need to change the save and load routines to use BPUT# and BGET# to store each character singly on to disk or tape. The advantage of these programs is that they do not eat into the RAM for program storage and so nearly all the remaining memory can be used for text.

This program does produce neat text, however, and the modules included in the procedures could be used as the basis for a detailed text storage program even if you don't have access to a printer. The print module is almost identical to the formatted text display module, except that naturally enough the line numbers do not appear.

If you choose to edit what you have entered, a sub-menu appears, with the option to delete a line entirely, or to alter it. If you choose to delete a line, all the subsequent lines move up one to take its place. If you wish to alter a line, the original appears on the screen and you can copy the sections that you need using the <COPY> key and the cursor control keys if this makes the task easier.

The saving and loading modules are fairly standard, consisting of a saved variable that denotes the number of elements in the array, followed by the array itself. Note that the array is stored as an array, not as single bytes.

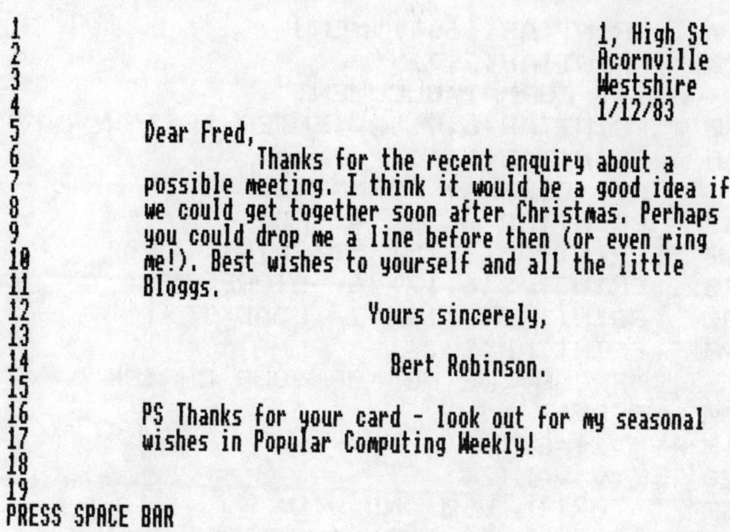

```
 1                                          1, High St
 2                                          Acornville
 3                                          Westshire
 4                                          1/12/83
 5     Dear Fred,
 6              Thanks for the recent enquiry about a
 7     possible meeting. I think it would be a good idea if
 8     we could get together soon after Christmas. Perhaps
 9     you could drop me a line before then (or even ring
10     me!). Best wishes to yourself and all the little
11     Bloggs.
12                        Yours sincerely,
13
14                        Bert Robinson.
15
16        PS Thanks for your card - look out for my seasonal
17        wishes in Popular Computing Weekly!
18
19
PRESS SPACE BAR
```

Figure 2.3: Screen Dump from Texted.

In this program, most of the requirements seem to have been satisfied. Those that have not, include a word count and a search routine. These routines will reduce the amount of memory available for text storage but, if found necessary, the word count could be achieved from the menu by looping through all the array and counting the number of spaces and carriage returns. A suitable search and replace routine would use the INSTR function to look for an occurrence of an entered string and would use the returned value to delete the original string and substitute the replacement. This should not prove too difficult to implement and is left as homework!

Texted

```
1000 REM **        TEXTED      **
1010 REM
1020 REM **   AJS 1/12/83 **
1030
1040 PROC_init
1050
1060 REPEAT
1070    *FX15,0
1080    MODE3
1090    VDU19,0,6;0;
1100    VDU19,1,0;0;
```

```
1110      PRINTTAB(16,4)"MENU"
1120      PRINTTAB(6,7)
          "1. FORMAT DOCUMENT"
1130      PRINTTAB(6,9)"2. ENTER TEXT"
1140      PRINTTAB(6,11)
          "3. DISPLAY FORMATTED TEXT"
1150      PRINTTAB(6,13)"4. EDIT TEXT"
1160      PRINTTAB(6,15)"5. PRINT TEXT"
1170      PRINTTAB(6,17)"6. STORE TEXT"
1180      PRINTTAB(6,19)"7. LOAD TEXT"
1190      PRINTTAB(2,21)
          "PRESS THE NO. OF YOUR CHOICE"
1200      REPEAT
1210        Z$=GET$
1220        V=VAL(Z$)
1230        UNTIL V>0 AND V<8
1240      IFV=1 THEN PROC_format
1250      IFV=2 THEN PROC_input
1260      IFV=3 THEN MODE3:PROC_display
1270      IFV=4 THEN PROC_edit
1280      IFV=5 THEN MODE3:PROC_print
1290      IFV=6 THEN PROC_save
1300      IFV=7 THEN PROC_load
1310      UNTIL FALSE
1320
1330 DEFPROC_input
1340 CLS
1350 FORN=1TOlineno%-1
1360      PRINTA$(N)
1370      NEXT N
1380 flag%=0:jumpout=FALSE
1390 REPEAT
1400      letno%=1:spacepos%=0
1410      IF flag%<>0THEN letno%=letno%+
          LEN(A$(lineno%)):flag%=0
1420      REPEAT
1430        REPEAT
1440          Z$=GET$
1450          PRINTZ$;
1460          IF Z$="#" THEN jumpout=TRUE
1470          IFZ$=" " THEN spacepos%=
              letno%
1480          IF ASC(Z$)=127 OR jumpout=
              TRUE THEN letno%=letno%-1:
```

```
              GOTO1500
1490          A$(lineno%)=A$(lineno%)+Z$
1500          IF ASC(Z$)=127 THEN
              A$(lineno%)=
              LEFT$(A$(lineno%),letno%-1)
1510          UNTIL ASC(Z$)<>127
1520       letno%=letno%+1
1530       IF Z$=CHR$(13) AND letno%<
           linelength THEN flag%=1:PRINT
1540       IF LEN(A$(lineno%))>linelength
           -1 THEN flag%=2
1550       UNTIL flag%<>0 OR jumpout=TRUE
1560     len=LEN(A$(lineno%))-spacepos%
1570     lastword$=
         RIGHT$(A$(lineno%),len)
1580     IF flag%=2 THEN A$(lineno%+1)=
         lastword$
1590     IF flag%=2 THEN A$(lineno%)=
         LEFT$(A$(lineno%),spacepos%)
1600     lineno%=lineno%+1
1610     UNTIL lineno%=100 ORjumpout=TRUE
1620 ENDPROC
1630
1640 DEFPROC_display
1650 FOR N=1 TO lineno%
1660    PRINT STR$(N),TAB(leftmar)A$(N)
1670    IF lnspace>1THENPRINT
1680    IF lnspace>2THENPRINT
1690    IF lineno% MOD (lines-14) <>0
        THEN 1740
1700    FOR S=1 TO 14
1710       PRINT
1720       NEXT S
1730    PRINT
1740    NEXT N
1750 PRINT"PRESS SPACE BAR"
1760 A$=GET$
1770 ENDPROC
1780
1790 DEFPROC_edit
1800 CLS
1810 PRINTTAB(16,4)"EDIT TEXT"
1820 PRINTTAB(6,7)"1. DELETE LINES"
1830 PRINTTAB(6,9)"2. CHANGE LINES"
```

```
1840 PRINTTAB(6,11)"PRESS 1 OR 2"
1850 REPEAT
1860    Z$ = GET$
1870    UNTIL Z$ = "1" OR Z$ = "2"
1880 IF Z$ = "1" THEN PROC_del ELSE
     PROC_change
1890 ENDPROC
1900
1910 DEFPROC_change
1920 PRINTTAB(6,14)
     "ENTER THE LINE NO. TO CHANGE"
1930 INPUT changeno%
1940 PRINTA$(changeno%)
1950 PRINTTAB(6,18)"ENTER THE NEW LINE"
1960 REPEAT
1970   PRINTTAB(0,19)STRING$(40," ")
1980   PRINTTAB(0,18)
1990   A$(changeno%)=""
2000   REPEAT
2010     Z$ = GET$
2020     PRINTZ$;
2030     A$(changeno%)=A$(changeno%)+Z$
2040     UNTIL Z$=CHR$(13)
2042   D$=A$(changeno%)
2045   dlen=LEN(D$)
2046   dlen=LEN(D$)
2048   A$(changeno%)=LEFT$(D$,dlen-1)
2050   PRINTTAB(0,21)STRING$(40," ");
2060   PRINTTAB(0,21)"IS THIS CORRECT?"
2070   Z$ = GET$
2080   PRINTTAB(0,21)STRING$(40," ");
2090   UNTIL Z$ = "Y" OR Z$ = "y"
2100 ENDPROC
2110
2120 DEFPROC_del
2130 PRINTTAB(6,14)
     "ENTER THE LINE NO. TO DELETE"
2140 INPUT delno%
2150 FOR N = delno% TO lineno%-1
2160   A$(N)=A$(N+1)
2170   NEXT N
2180 lineno%=lineno%-1 AND lineno%>1
2190 ENDPROC
2200
```

```
2210 DEFPROC_print
2220 VDU2
2230 FOR N=1 TO lineno%
2240    PRINTTAB(leftmar)A$(N)
2250    IF lnspace>1THENPRINT
2260    IF lnspace>2THENPRINT
2270    IF lineno% MOD (lines-14) <> 0
       THEN 2310
2280    FOR S=1 TO 14
2290       PRINT
2300       NEXT S
2310    NEXT N
2320 VDU3
2330 PRINT"PRESS SPACE BAR"
2340 A$=GET$
2350 ENDPROC
2360
2370 DEFPROC_init
2380 lineno%=1
2390 linelength=55
2400 leftmar=12
2410 lines=66
2420 lnspace=1
2430 DIMA$(100)
2440 ENDPROC
2450
2460 DEFPROC_format
2470 LOCAL V
2480 CLS
2490 PRINTTAB(16,2)"FORMATTING"
2500 PRINTTAB(13,3)"****************"
2510 PRINTTAB(5,5)
     "HOW MANY CHARACTERS PER LINE?"
2520 PRINTTAB(5,7)
     "(DEFAULT = "linelength")";
2530 INPUT A$
2540 V=VAL A$
2550 IF A$<>"" AND V>10 AND V<81 THEN
     linelength=V
2560 PRINTTAB(5,9)"LEFT MARGIN?"
2570 PRINTTAB(5,11)
     "(DEFAULT = "leftmar")";
2580 INPUT A$
2590 V=VAL A$
```

```
2600 IF A$<>"" AND V>0 AND
     V<80-linelength THEN leftmar=V
2610 PRINTTAB(5,13)
     "HOW MANY LINES PER PAGE"
2620 PRINTTAB(5,15)
     "(DEFAULT = "lines")";
2630 INPUT A$
2640 V=VAL A$
2650 IF A$<>"" AND V>20 AND V<80 THEN
     lines=60
2660 PRINTTAB(5,17)
     "ENTER LINESPACING (1 to 3)"
2670 PRINTTAB(5,19)
     "(DEFAULT = "lnspace")";
2680 INPUT A$
2690 V=VAL A$
2700 IF A$<>"" AND V>0 AND V<4 THEN
     lnspace=V
2710 PRINTTAB(5,21)"PRESS SPACE BAR"
2720 A$=GET$
2730 ENDPROC
2740
2750 DEFPROC_save
2760 CLS
2770 PRINTTAB(5,5)
     "ENTER THE NAME OF THE FILE"
2780 PRINTTAB(10,7)"YOU WISH TO SAVE"
2790 INPUT file$
2800 channel%=OPENOUT(file$)
2810 PRINT#channel%,lineno%
2820 FORN=1TOlineno%
2830    PRINT# channel%,A$(N)
2840    NEXT N
2850   CLOSE# channel%
2860 ENDPROC
2870
2880 DEFPROC_load
2890 lineno%=100
2900 CLS
2910 PRINTTAB(5,5)
     "ENTER THE NAME OF THE FILE"
2920 PRINTTAB(10,7)"YOU WISH TO LOAD"
2930 INPUT file$
2940 flen%=100
```

```
2950 channel%=OPENIN(file$)
2960 INPUT#channel%,lineno%
2970 FORN=1TOlineno%
2980    INPUT# channel%,A$(N)
2990    NEXT N
3000 CLOSE# channel%
3010 ENDPROC
```

Notes on the program

Line 1040 sends control to the initialising routine.

Lines 1060–1310 contain the menu, and would normally be contained in a procedure. Originally this section was in mode 6, and you cannot change modes within a procedure. If your display is clear enough on a TV, you can leave the program in mode 3 for text entering. If it is difficult to read, **line 1080** should be changed to read MODE6.

Line 1070 flushes all internal buffers so that the option choice is not influenced by earlier keypresses.

Line 1090 turns the background to cyan, and **line 1100** turns the foreground to black — a change from the familiar blue and white of most of the text programs in this book. The rest of this module is standard display of a menu, and a routine to accept choices between 1 and 7.

PROC_input is probably the most complex in the program and controls how text is entered and stored in a partially formatted form.

Lines 1350–1370 print the text that has been entered so far. Variable lineno% contains the number of lines input so far.

Line 1380 sets two flags to 0. These are used to check if the line length has been reached or if the user is jumping out of entry mode.

Line 1390 starts a loop that continues until either the maximum number of lines has been reached or the user has chosen to jump out.

Line 1420 starts a loop that continues until the line length has been exceeded or the user has chosen to jump out.

Line 1430 starts a loop that continues to **line 1510** and loops if the key pressed has an ASCII code of 127 — <DELETE>. Variable letno% contains the value of the letter number in the string.

Line 1440 reads the keyboard and loads the value into variable Z$ which is printed on the screen by **line 1450**.

Line 1460 checks Z$ to see if a '#' has been entered. **Lines 1470–1500** deal with the case when <DELETE> has been pressed. **Line 1490** adds Z$ to A$(N), the array that stores the line.

Line 1530 sets flag% to 1 if <RETURN> has been pressed. **Line 1540** sets flag% to 2 if the line length has been reached.

Variable spacepos% contains the position of the last space entered. This is needed to move the last complete word to the next line.

Lines 1560–1600 control the movement of the word to the next line and **line 1600** increases the value of lineno% by 1 so that the word is stored in the next element of the array.

PROC_display displays all the lines in the array A$. **Line 1660** prints the line numbers as a string. If the line simply said PRINT N, etc, then the line numbers would move in by about eight positions. Using STR$ ensures that the numbers are up against the lefthand edge of the screen.

Variable 'leftmar' determines the left margin for the text.

Lines 1670 and **1680** control the spacing between lines.

Lines 1690–1730 check to see if the bottom of the page has been reached. If it has, empty print lines are used to move the print position to the top of the next page.

PROC_edit puts a small menu on the screen, allowing the choice of either deleting or altering lines. Before using this module, it is important to look at the formatted text so as to find the number of the lines that need action.

PROC_change is fairly simple and displays the existing line on the screen. The new line is entered and can be checked until it is correct. If formatting errors occur during printing, they may be due to the string containing delete codes. These will not show up on the screen but might be intercepted by the printer. Using the edit facility, a fresh line can be entered.

PROC_del needs the line number to be input, and then the subsequent lines move up by one position to effectively remove all trace of it.

Line 2180 is a short form of 'if the number of lines is greater than one then reduce the number by one'. This line is to prevent an attempt to call a negative element in the array, which cannot of course exist.

PROC_print is similar to PROC_display except that there are no line numbers sent to the printer. **Line 2220** sends output to the printer as well as to the screen and **line 2320** turns the printer off.

PROC_init sets the formatting variables to their initial values and reserves space for the text. At present it is set to 100 lines of text but can be set considerably higher if required. If you forego the facility of seeing the text in its final form on the screen in mode 3, the whole program could be in mode 6 which would release a further 8K of storage space.

PROC_format provides a menu to select formatting requirements. If <RETURN> is pressed with no input, the values remain the same.

Remember that changing the number of characters in a line only affects text input after the command and cannot alter text already stored.

PROC_save and **PROC_load** are typical save and load routines and store the number of lines as well as the text array itself. The text can be given suitable names for storage, up to 10 characters in length when using cassettes and up to seven characters when using disks.

CHAPTER 3
Characters and Plots in Display

The screen display

One of the reasons that people choose to buy an Electron or a BBC micro is because they are machines with excellent graphics. Most home computers are now capable of producing high resolution pictures using a range of colours, but many involve direct addressing of the memory. Acorn machines score in having a wide range of easy commands in BASIC.

When you read through the manual, you may be a little puzzled by some of the commands, and the fact that the PLOT statement has an awful lot of variations. If you learn just a few of the drawing commands when you start programming, you will find that you can achieve most of the things you require with these, and gradually use more as your needs increase. If you look at other people's listings you will probably find that they don't use more than three or four different drawing commands in their programs. One way to understand this is to compare it with the fact that there are 100,000 words in most languages, but you can make yourself understood with just 600.

Before we look at the drawing side of graphics, it is a good idea to see how everything appears on the screen. There are five modes available on Electrons and BBC B machines that will support graphics and text: 0, 1, 2, 4 and 6. There are two that will support only text: 3 and 6. (I shall not consider teletext mode 7 on the BBC, as that is a special case and gets its characters in a different way to all the other modes.)

Modes 2 and 5 produce 20 characters to the line, modes 1 and 4 produce 40 characters, and modes 0 and 3, 80 characters. Each character is formed on a matrix or grid of 8×8 pixels (or dots), and each row of dots has a code number. This number (which makes up one eighth of the definition of the character) is stored in permanent memory and is read when the character needs to be printed on the screen. The letter A looks like **Figure 3.1** on the screen.

Each dot is represented by a one, and the spaces by zeros. The row of dots and spaces has now become an eight-digit binary number. Although this is fine for the computer, it is easier for human beings if the number is turned into base 10, or into a hexadecimal (base 16) number. This produces eight numbers that together give a definition for the letter.

```
BASE 10          BINARY           PIXELS

    60           00111100
   102           01100110
   102           01100110
   126           01111110
   102           01100110
   102           01100110
   102           01100110
     0           00000000
```

Figure 3.1: The Letter A.

For instance, if the numbers were all 255, the result would be a solid block: to produce a space, you would need eight zeros. From this you can see that you don't have to stop with letters — any shape, including space invaders, little figures, etc, that fit on an 8 × 8 grid can be coded. The computer stores these codes at memory positions starting at &0C00, and you can peek into them to see if these numbers are there. The following program does just that — you enter the ASCII code of the character you wish to look at and the definition appears in large form on the screen, eg letter A has the ASCII code 65.

Character View

```
1000 REM ** CHARACTER VIEW **
1010
1020 REM ** A.J.S. 4/10/83 **
1030
1040 REM Define background
1050 MODE1
1060 VDU19,0,4;0;
1070
1080 REM Define solid character
1090 VDU23,225,255,255,255,255,255,255,
     255,255
1100
1110 REM Dimension array to hold nos
1120 DIMZ(8)
1130
1140 REPEAT
1150    CLS
1160    PRINT
1170    PRINT"ENTER THE CHARACTER NO."
1180    PRINT"YOU WISH TO SEE DISPLAYED"
1190    REPEAT
```

```
1200        PRINTTAB(0,3)"      "
1210        INPUTTAB(0,3)charnum
1220       UNTIL charnum>32 AND
           charnum<127
1230     PRINT"WHICH IS "CHR$(charnum)
1240     PRINT
1250     REM Input loop to hold 8 numbers
1260     FORX=1 TO 8
1270       Z(X) =
           ?(&C000+(charnum-32)*8+X-1)
1280       NEXT X
1290     PRINT
1300     PRINT"BASE 10"TAB(15)"BINARY",
         "PIXELS"
1310     PRINT
1320
1330     REM Loop for each character line
1340     FORP=1TO8
1350       A=Z(P)
1360       A$="":REM Holds solid
                 blocks of character
1370       B$="":REM Holds binary
                 equivalent of each line
1380       FORN=7TO0STEP-1
1390         B=INT(A/2^N)
1400         IF B=1 THENA$=A$+CHR$(225)
             ELSE A$ = A$+" "
1410         IF B=1 THENB$=B$+"1"
             ELSE B$ = B$+"0"
1420         C=A MOD 2^N
1430         A=C
1440         NEXT N
1450       PRINTTAB(2)STR$(Z(P))
           TAB(15)B$,A$
1460       NEXT P
1470     PRINT
1480     PRINT"PRESS SPACE BAR TO REPEAT"
1490     Z$=GET$
1500     UNTIL FALSE
```

Notes on the program

Line 1060 sets the colour to blue.

   Line 1090 defines a solid block — note that either 255 or the hex equivalent, &FF, could be used here. The binary form is 11111111.

Lines 1190–1220 only allow you to look at characters between 32 and 126. This is the range of characters that is stored.

Lines 1260–1280 store the character definition in an array, Z(X).

Line 1300 prints column headings. Using commas between each section utilizes the automatic tabulation to spread them out.

Lines 1340–1460 convert the stored numbers into their binary equivalent and into strings of solid blocks and spaces. **Lines 1380–1440** convert to binary by successively dividing the number by powers of 2, starting with 2 to the power of 7 (128), then dividing the remainder by the next smallest power, until it reaches 2 to the power of 1, ie 2 itself.

If the number can be divided, a 1 is added to the string B$ and a solid block to string A$. **Line 1450** prints the finished line of ones and zeros as well as a row of blocks and spaces.

Defining your own alphabet

Just as it is easy to look at the characters stored in the computer, so it is simple to change the definitions of existing characters. There is no point in doing this, however, as there are special characters reserved for this purpose, between 224 and 255. Although you can redefine any character number, using these numbers will not take up any more memory. You define letters simply by using the VDU 23 statement as follows:

VDU 23, 225, 255, 255, 255, 255, 255, 255, 255, 255

This will define CHR$225 as a solid block. If you now enter:

PRINT CHR$225

you will see a large block printed on the screen. (This will work in all six modes on the Electron and all modes except for mode 7 on the BBC micro.)

The next program asks you for the number of the character you wish to redefine and then you have to enter the eight numbers that make up the new definition. As you can see, it is largely based on the last program.

Define New Characters

```
1000 REM **   DEFINE NEW CHARACTERS   **
1010
1020 REM **      A.J.S. 4/10/83       **
1030
```

```
1040  REM Define background
1050  MODE1
1060  VDU19,0,4;0;
1070
1080  REM Define solid character
1090  VDU23,225,255,255,255,255,255,255,
      255,255
1100
1110  REM Dimension array to hold nos
1120  DIMZ(8)
1130
1140  REPEAT
1150    CLS
1160    PRINT
1170    PRINT
      "ENTER THE NO. OF THE CHARACTER"
1180    PRINT "YOU WISH TO REDEFINE   "
1190    REPEAT
1200      PRINTTAB(0,3)"        "
1210      INPUTTAB(0,3)charnum
1220      UNTIL charnum>225 AND
      charnum<256
1230    PRINT
1240    REM Input loop to hold 8 numbers
1250    PRINT
      "NOW ENTER THE NO. OF EACH ROW"
1260    FORX=1TO8
1270      PRINT"ROW "X;
1280      INPUTZ(X)
1290      NEXT X
1300    PRINT
1310    PRINT"BASE 10"TAB(15)"BINARY",
      "PIXELS"
1320    PRINT
1330
1340    REM Loop for each character line
1350    FORP=1TO8
1360      A=Z(P)
1370      A$="":REM Holds solid
              blocks of character
1380      B$="":REM Holds binary
              equivalent of each line
1390      FORN=7TO0STEP-1
1400        B=INT(A/2^N)
```

```
1410          IF B=1 THEN A$=A$+CHR$(225)
              ELSE A$ = A$+" "
1420          IF B=1 THEN B$=B$+"1"
              ELSE B$ = B$+"0"
1430          C=A MOD 2^N
1440          A=C
1450          NEXT N
1460        PRINTTAB(2)STR$(Z(P))
            TAB(15)B$,A$
1470        NEXT P
1480      PRINT
1490      PRINT"IS THIS CORRECT?"
1500      REPEAT
1510        Z$=GET$
1520        UNTILZ$="Y" OR Z$="N"
1530      IF Z$ = "Y" THEN VDU23,charnum,
          Z(1),Z(2),Z(3),Z(4),Z(5),
          Z(6),Z(7),Z(8)
1540      PRINT
1550      IF Z$="Y" THEN PRINT"CHARACTER "
          charnum" is "CHR$(charnum)
1560      PRINT
1570      PRINT"PRESS SPACE BAR TO REPEAT"
1580      Z$=GET$
1590      UNTIL FALSE
```

Notes on the program

Lines 1190–1220 allow you to redefine characters with an ASCII code of 226 to 255. You can change the limits here to allow you to redefine the normal character set from 32 upwards, but you will get odd results as the text in the program will become corrupted. Pressing <BREAK> then entering OLD will restore things to normal.

Lines 1260–1290 allow the input of eight numbers to define the new character.

Line 1490 allows you to check to see if you like the result. If you do, then **line 1530** uses the values in a VDU23 statement to permanently store the new character. A standard size version is also shown. Characters that you enter in this manner will remain in future programs until you press <BREAK> or switch off the computer.

Sideways characters

The last program allowed you to alter the character set or to define new letters. One occasion when you might need different letters is if you are trying to label a display from top to bottom. Although in the case of graphs you can print letters on top of each other, it would be useful to have a character set lying on its side to increase legibility.

CHARACTER ROTATE

****

ABCDEFGHIJKLMNOPQRSTUVWXYZ

PRESS SPACE BAR TO REPEAT

Figure 3.2: Screen Dump from Character Rotate.

To save time writing your own definitions, you can use those already stored in the computer, and simply rearrange the character matrix. This is what the next program sets out to do, and it uses techniques from the previous two programs.

Character Rotate

```
1000 REM ** CHARACTER ROTATE **
1010
1020 REM **   A.J.S. 4/10/83   **
1030
1040 REM Define background
1050 MODE1
1060 VDU19,0,4;0;
1070
1080 REM Define solid character
1090 VDU23,225,255,255,255,255,255,255,
     255,255
1100
1110 REM Dimension array to hold nos
1120 DIMZ(8)
1130 DIMC$(8,8)
1140 DIMD(8)
1150
1160 REPEAT
1170   CLS
1180   PRINT
1190   PRINTTAB(12,2)"CHARACTER ROTATE"
```

```
1200    PRINTTAB(0,4)STRING$(40,"*")
1210    PRINTTAB(7);
1220    FOR charnum=65 TO 90
1230      PRINTCHR$(charnum);
1240      NEXT charnum
1250    PRINTTAB(7,8);
1260    FOR charnum=65 TO 90
1270      FORX=1 TO 8
1280        Z(X) =
             ?(&C000+(charnum-32)*8+X-1)
1290        NEXT X
1300      FORP=1TO8
1310        A=Z(P)
1320        FORN=7TO0STEP-1
1330          B=INT(A/2^N)
1340          IF B=1 THEN C$(N,P)="1"
                ELSE C$(N,P)="0"
1350          C=A MOD 2^N
1360          A=C
1370          NEXT N
1380        NEXT P
1390      FOR Z=0TO7
1400        D(Z)=0
1410        FOR Y=1TO8
1420          D(Z)=D(Z)+VAL(C$(Z,Y))*
              2^(8-Y)
1430          NEXT Y
1440        NEXT Z
1450      VDU23,charnum+159,D(0),D(1),
          D(2),D(3),D(4),D(5),D(6),D(7)
1460      PRINTCHR$(charnum+159);
1470      NEXT charnum
1480    PRINT
1490    PRINT"PRESS SPACE BAR TO REPEAT"
1500    Z$=GET$
1510    UNTIL FALSE
```

Notes on the program

Lines 1220–1240 print out the normal upper case character set. **Line 1210** simply moves the cursor to the starting position for the line.

Lines 1260–1470 contain a large loop to deal with all 26 letters. **Lines 1270–1290** read the character definitions from the normal character set for each letter and load them into array Z(X).

Lines 1300–1380 convert the numbers into a string array, C$(Z,Y), containing the binary equivalent of ones and zeros. **Lines 1390–1440** read the first character of each element of Z(X) into a new array, D(Z). This is repeated for the second character and so on until the whole array has been converted.

Line 1450 uses VDU23 to store each new definition. **Line 1460** prints the resultant character under the original line, but all the characters are now lying on their backs.

As before, this new character set remains inside the computer, even when a new program has been loaded. To save the new definitions, it is possible to use the save routine from the next program.

Drawing a character on the screen

One disadvantage with the method employed in the last program is that you need to sketch out the new character on a piece of paper, then calculate the ones and zeros, and then convert them into base 10 before you can form the new character. It would be a lot easier to draw the character on a large grid on the screen, entering and rubbing out where necessary as you alter the shape and try out new ideas.

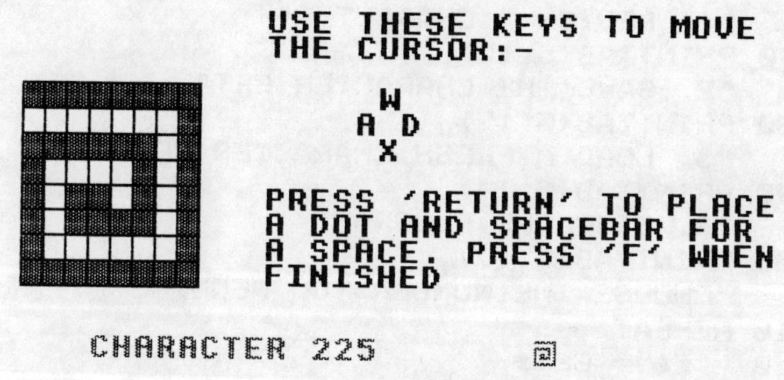

Figure 3.3: Screen Dump from Character Designer.

This is achieved in the next program by having a grid with a flashing cursor to move around. When you want a pixel filled in, you press <RETURN>, and when you want a space, you press the space bar. You are shown the characters that are already defined, you can alter any you wish, and you can view them in their small and large sizes. An added refinement is the ability to save the new definitions on tape or disk, and load them in again at a later date. What's more, you don't even dirty your hands by using ASCII codes or VDU numbers — it's all contained in the program.

Character Designer

```
1000 REM   ***   CHARACTER DESIGNER   ***
1010 REM
1020 REM   ***        AJS 10/9/83        ***
1030
1040 MODE1
1050 DIM L(8)
1060 VDU19,0,4;0;
1070
1080 REPEAT
1090    PROC_menu
1100    UNTIL FALSE
1110
1120 DEFPROC_menu
1130 CLS
1140 PRINTTAB(8,1)"CHARACTER DESIGNER"
1150 PRINTTAB(5,5)"YOU CAN:-"
1160 PRINTTAB(5,8)
        "1. DESIGN A CHARACTER"
1170 PRINTTAB(5,10)
        "2. SAVE THE CHARACTER SET"
1180 PRINTTAB(5,12)
        "3. LOAD A FRESH CHARACTER SET"
1190 PRINTTAB(5,14)
        "4. STOP THE PROGRAM"
1200 PRINTTAB(5,17)
        "CHOOSE THE NUMBER YOU REQUIRE"
1210 REPEAT
1220    Z$ = GET$
1230    UNTIL VAL(Z$)>0 AND VAL(Z$)<5
1240 IF Z$="1" THEN PROC_design
1250 IF Z$="2" THEN PROC_save
1260 IF Z$="3" THEN PROC_load
1270 IF Z$="4" THEN STOP
1280 ENDPROC
1290
1300 DEFPROC_design
```

```
1310 PROC_init
1320 PROC_instruct
1330 PROC_main
1340 ENDPROC
1350
1360 DEFPROC_init
1370 VDU23,224,0,&7F,&7F,&7F,&7F,&7F,
     &7F,&7F
1380 A=128
1390 B=768
1400 R=1
1410 C=1
1420 FOR N = 1 TO 8
1430    L(N) = 0
1440    NEXT N
1450 ENDPROC
1460
1470 DEFPROC_instruct
1480 *FX21,0
1490 CLS
1500 PRINTTAB(8,1)"CHARACTER DESIGNER"
1510 FORN=1 TO 15
1520    PRINTTAB(5,N+4)N+224,CHR$(N+224)
1530    NEXT N
1540 FORN=1 TO 15
1550    PRINTTAB(25,N+4)
        N+239,CHR$(N+239)
1560    NEXT N
1570 REPEAT
1580    PRINTTAB(0,24)STRING$(20,CHR$32)
1590    PRINTTAB(5,22)
        "ENTER THE NO. OF THE CHARACTER"
1600    PRINTTAB(5,23)
        "YOU WISH TO REDEFINE"
1610    INPUT chrno
1620    UNTIL chrno>224 AND chrno<255
1630 ENDPROC
1640
1650 DEFPROC_main
1660 PROC_screen
1670 VDU5
1680 REPEAT
1690    GCOL3,2
1700    IF INKEY(-51) AND A<352 THEN
```

```
        A=A+32:C=C+1:REM D
1710    IF INKEY(-66) AND A>128 THEN
        A=A-32:C=C-1:REM A
1720    IF INKEY(-34) AND B<768 THEN
        B=B+32:R=R-1:REM W
1730    IF INKEY(-67) AND B>544 THEN
        B=B-32:R=R+1:REM X
1740    MOVEA,B
1750    PRINTCHR$224
1760    MOVEA,B
1770    PRINTCHR$224
1780    IF INKEY(-74) THEN PROC_dot
1790    IF INKEY(-99) THEN PROC_blank
1800    VDU23,chrno,L(1),L(2),L(3),L(4),
        L(5),L(6),L(7),L(8)
1810    MOVE230,450
1820    GCOL0,2
1830    PRINT"CHARACTER ";chrno,
        CHR$(chrno)
1840    UNTIL INKEY(-68)
1850 VDU4
1860 ENDPROC
1870
1880 DEFPROC_screen
1890 CLS
1900 PRINTTAB(8,1)"CHARACTER DESIGNER"
1910 FOR X = 128 TO 384 STEP 32
1920    MOVEX,512:PLOT1,0,256
1930    NEXT X
1940 FOR Y = 512 TO 768 STEP 32
1950    MOVE128,Y:PLOT1,256,0
1960    NEXT Y
1970 VDU28,15,18,39,5
1980 PRINT"USE THESE KEYS TO MOVE"
1990 PRINT"THE CURSOR:-"
2000 PRINT
2010 PRINT"     W"
2020 PRINT"    A D"
2030 PRINT"     X"
2040 PRINT
2050 PRINT"PRESS 'RETURN' TO PLACE"
2060 PRINT"A DOT AND SPACEBAR FOR"
2070 PRINT"A SPACE. PRESS 'F' WHEN"
2080 PRINT"FINISHED"
```

```
2090 VDU26
2100 ENDPROC
2110
2120 DEFPROC_dot
2130 MOVEA,B
2140 GCOL0,2
2150 PRINTCHR$224
2160 L(R)=L(R)OR2^(8-C)
2170 ENDPROC
2180
2190 DEFPROC_blank
2200 MOVE230,450
2210 PRINT"CHARACTER ";chrno,
     CHR$(chrno)
2220 MOVE A,B
2230 GCOL3,2
2240 PRINTCHR$224
2250 L(R)=L(R)AND255-2^(8-C)
2260 ENDPROC
2270
2280 DEFPROC_save
2290 A%=131
2300 X=USR(&FFF4)
2310 Y=X+240
2320 *SAVE "chars" C00 CFF
2330 ENDPROC
2340
2350 DEFPROC_load
2360 *LOAD "chars"
2370 ENDPROC
```

Notes on the program

Lines 1040–1060 set the mode and dimension array space to store the new numbers for the character definition. **Line 1080** puts the menu routine in an endless loop.

PROC_menu provides four choices — define new characters, save or load new character sets, and stop.

PROC_design sends program control to three other procedures.

PROC_init defines character 224 as a solid block slightly smaller than the complete 8 × 8 matrix. Variables A and B hold the position of the cursor. **Line 1480** clears the keyboard buffer.

PROC_instruct accepts input of the required character number. If you alter the limits to the number here, you run the risk of corrupting other data, as well as the normal character set. If you need more space for extra characters, you can use *FX20,1 to explode the memory allocation as explained in page 282 of the Electron User Guide and page 427 in the BBC User Guide.

PROC_screen explains the use of certain keys to move the cursor and sets up a text window in **line 1970**.
    Line 1670 uses VDU5 to allow printing to take place at the graphics cursor. If you entered MOVE 100,100:PRINT "HELLO", the word HELLO would appear at position 100,100 on the screen.
    Line 1840 sends the program back to the REPEAT in **line 1680** unless the letter F has been pressed. **Line 1850** uses VDU4 to make text appear at the text and not the graphics cursor, ie it switches off the effect of VDU5.
    Lines 1700–1730 use INKEY to see if W, X, A or D have been pressed. **Lines 1780** and **1790** check to see if the <RETURN> key or the space bar has been pressed. **Line 1800** defines the new character using VDU23. **Lines 1910–1960** draw the grid in which the new character is designed. **Line 2090** sets the text window back to its normal size.

PROC_dot uses GCOL 0,2 to plot the solid block at the positions set by A and B.

PROC_blank prints a solid block as in PROC_dot. It then plots over the top with GCOL 3,2. This is an example of exclusive OR plotting, and is a good way to remove characters that have been plotted.
    Lines 2160 and **2250** change the value of L(R) according to whether there is a solid block or a space present. These two lines use logical operators AND and OR to set particular bits to a zero or a one. This method is explained in some detail in Chapter 2, in the program Chef.

PROC_save uses an OSBYTE call to read the top of the operating system, with A% set to 131. This produces the address of the first free location above the operating system. The numbers C00 and CFF are the hexadecimal addresses of the start and finish of the block to be saved.

PROC_load loads in the fresh character set. If you are using a disk system and want to load and save several new character sets, it would be sensible to add a line in PROC_save and PROC_load to allow for your own filename to be input. In the version shown here, the character set is always known as 'chars'.

Extended graphics

Although it is possible to design programs that only use defined characters for illustration, there is far more that can be achieved using the extended graphics commands that are available. As was mentioned earlier, there are many different versions of the PLOT statement. PLOT is followed by three parameters, PLOT n,x,y. The x and y values control the screen positions, and the n value determines how the line is drawn — move, plot, dotted line, fill, etc.

The screen itself is divided into 1280 positions horizontally and 1024 positions vertically. The coordinates that make up the screen address 0,0 are positioned at the bottom lefthand corner. Acorn machines will not complain if you attempt to plot off the screen — the line will disappear off the edge, but the computer will act as if it is still plotting. The screen acts like a viewing window over a much larger area.

The most common versions of PLOT are PLOT 4,x,y and PLOT 5,x,y. Because these are used most frequently, they have simpler alternative names — MOVE and DRAW. Here are some useful PLOTs and what they do:

PLOT 1:   Move relative to last point.
PLOT 2:   Draw line relative to last point.
PLOT 4:   Move to absolute point.
PLOT 5:   Draw to absolute point.
PLOT 20:   Draw dotted line to absolute point.
PLOT 77:   Fill sideways from absolute point.
PLOT 85:   Fill a triangle from x,y to last two points visited.

The PLOT statements go up in multiples of eight according to their effect. For instance, PLOT 1, PLOT 9 and PLOT 17, etc, all control relative movement. In other words, using PLOT 1, 10, 20 will draw a line from the last point plotted to a point 10 units to the right and 20 units up. The statements PLOT 5, PLOT 13 and PLOT 21, etc, all control absolute movement. PLOT 5, 10, 20 will draw a line from the last point plotted to a point with screen coordinates 10,20.

Armed with this information, you could draw pictures on the screen quite simply by using direct statements. This series of instructions will draw a square:

MOVE 200, 200
DRAW 200, 0

```
DRAW 200, 0
DRAW 200, 200
DRAW 0, 200
DRAW 0, 0
```

You could, of course, put line numbers before the instructions and turn this into a short program. This is not using the capabilities of your computer to the full, however. There are many facilities that can be incorporated to make the program much more interesting. The next program continuously checks to see if any keys from a selection have been pressed. If they have, program control is sent to procedures that are in charge of different effects, eg cursor movement, colour, saving and loading.

For control of movement, a group of keys on the lefthand side of the keyboard has been chosen rather than the cursor keys.

```
    W
A   D
    X
```

This is because the cursor keys are not laid out on a separate pad, and most people find an arrangement like this a lot easier. If you would prefer to use other keys, it is simple to alter the program to your own specification.

Another feature of this program is the use of an array to hold all the keyboard presses. Each time a key is pressed, the ASCII code of that key is stored in the array $A\%(N)$. This means that at any time you can choose to stop the plotting, clear the screen and 'replay' what you have stored so far. Pressing another key will stop the array being emptied, and let you continue from that point. The advantage here is that, if you make a mistake, you can replot everything up until the point where you made the mistake.

You can also save the contents of the array to tape or disk at any time or load in previously saved pictures. This means that a design can be drawn in one corner of the screen, saved to tape and, after the cursor has been moved, plotted in several other positions on the screen.

It can be seen that the array is dimensioned to just over 1000 elements. If REMs are removed, it is possible to increase this by a certain amount, but if you want to store two or three thousand instructions in a complex design, you will have to sacrifice colour choice and use a less memory-hungry mode.

Sketch

```
1000 REM   *** SKETCH ***
1010 REM
```

```
1020 REM  *** A.J.S. ***
1030
1040 *TV255,1
1050 MODE2
1060 PROC_frame
1070 VDU28,0,31,19,28
1080 VDU23;8202;0;0;0;
1090 PROC_main
1100 STOP
1110
1120 DEFPROC_main
1130 DIMA%(1025)
1140 Z%=0
1150 REPEAT
1160    *FX15,0
1170    Z%=Z%+1
1180    N%=GET
1190    PROC_decode
1200    IF N%<75 OR N%>77 A%(Z%)=N%
1210    PLOT69,X%,Y%:PLOT70,X%,Y%
1220    IFZ%=1000PRINT '
       "ALMOST OUT OF MEMORY"
1230    PRINTTAB(0,0)Z%
1240    UNTILZ%=1050
1250 PRINT ' "OUT OF MEMORY"
1260 GCOL0,7
1270 ENDPROC
1280
1290 DEFPROC_decode
1300 IF N%>47 AND N%<59THEN GCOL0,N%-48
1310 IF N%=65 THEN X%=X%-8:PROC_draw
1320 IF N%=68 THEN X%=X%+8:PROC_draw
1330 IF N%=88 THEN Y%=Y%-8:PROC_draw
1340 IF N%=87 THEN Y%=Y%+8:PROC_draw
1350 IF N%=69 THEN X%=X%+8:Y%=Y%+8:
     PROC_draw
1360 IF N%=90 THEN X%=X%-8:Y%=Y%-8:
     PROC_draw
1370 IF N%=81 THEN X%=X%-8:Y%=Y%+8:
     PROC_draw
1380 IF N%=67 THEN X%=X%+8:Y%=Y%-8:
     PROC_draw
1390 IF N%=76 THEN PROC_look
1400 IF N%=77 THEN PROC_save
```

```
1410 IF N%=75 THEN PROC_load
1420 ENDPROC
1430
1440 DEFPROC_draw
1450 IF X%<8 X%=8
1460 IF X%>1264 X%=1264
1470 IF Y%<132 Y%=132
1480 IF Y%>1012 Y%=1012
1490 PLOT5,X%,Y%
1500 ENDPROC
1510
1520 DEFPROC_frame
1530 MOVE0,128:DRAW0,1020:DRAW1272,1020
1540 DRAW1272,128:DRAW0,128
1550 MOVE640,560:X%=640:Y%=560:
     PROC_draw
1560 ENDPROC
1570
1580 DEFPROC_look
1590 CLG
1600 GCOL0,7
1610 PROC_frame
1620 D%=Z%
1630 FORL%=1TOZ%
1640    N%=A%(L%)
1650    PROC_decode
1660    PRINTTAB(0,0)(L%)
1670    S%=INKEY(0)
1680    IF S%= 83 THEN S%=INKEY(100)
1690    IF S%= 83 THEN Z%=L%:L%=D%
1700    NEXT
1710 ENDPROC
1720
1730 DEFPROC_save
1740 CLS
1750 INPUT ' "SAVING" '
     "ENTER A NAME-"file$
1760 x%=OPENOUT(file$)
1770 PRINT#x%,Z%
1780 FOR N=1TOZ%
1790    PRINT#x%,A%(N)
1800    NEXT N
1810 CLOSE#x%
1820 CLS
```

```
1830 ENDPROC
1840
1850 DEFPROC_load
1860 CLS
1870 INPUT ' "LOADING" '
        "ENTER A NAME-"file$
1880 x%=OPENIN(file$)
1890 INPUT#x%,Z%
1900 FOR N=1TOZ%
1910    INPUT#x%,A%(N)
1920    N%=A%(N):PROC_decode
1930    NEXT N
1940 CLOSE#x%
1950 CLS
1960 ENDPROC
```

Notes on the program

Line 1040 states *TV255,1. This line applies to the BBC computer only, and can be used as a direct statement or as a program line. It moves the display down the screen slightly and also turns off the interlacing, the flickering effect you get in modes 0 to 6.

As the Electron does not use the same graphics chip as the BBC machine, this does not work on the Electron. In programs for the Electron, it is wise to avoid using the top line of the display as it is sometimes unreadable.

Line 1070 defines a text window, and **line 1080** turns off the flashing cursor.

PROC_main dimensions some space for the array that holds the drawing commands that have been entered.

Line 1160 clears all buffers, just in case you have been idly tapping the keyboard. **Line 1180** waits for an input and goes to PROC_decode to have it interpreted. **Line 1200** checks to see if the keys pressed are ones that are used in this program. If they are, their codes are stored in the array A%.

This program uses mainly integer variables to increase the speed.

Line 1210 produces the flashing drawing cursor by alternately plotting and overplotting with the logical inverse colour.

PROC_decode checks which keys have been pressed and takes the appropriate action. If a number key has been pressed, the drawing colour changes. If keys used to control the cursor are pressed, control branches to PROC_draw. If L is pressed, then the program is sent to PROC_look; if M, the array so far is saved; and if K, a previous array is loaded.

PROC_draw defines the limits of the drawing area.

PROC_frame draws the outline of the drawing area.

PROC_look clears the graphics area and starts to use the stored plotting instructions to steer it round the screen. If a letter S is pressed during this period, the drawing will pause. If the key is again pressed in the next second, the array stops being loaded and control is sent back to PROC_ decode and PROC_main. This allows the user to load in just part of a stored array and to continue from that point.

PROC_save permits the entry of a filename and the number of keypress codes as well as the keypresses themselves are saved.

PROC_load operates in reverse but sends control to PROC_decode as it is being loaded so that the drawing appears on the screen.

Graphics design

The next program bases several of its routines on the previous program, but does not have the ability to save detailed instructions in an array. Instead, it provides a much wider range of features, including plot, move, colours, two-speed plotting, boxes and circles, outline or filled-in shapes and text on screen. These are the sort of features that would normally be found in a professional design utility, and make the program much faster to use. Due to the fact that there is only a limited amount of memory available, you have to decide which features you need in a graphics program. Unfortunately, you cannot combine arrays and easy shapes unless you forego the resolution or range of colours.

In the following program, there are two windows — an upper graphics screen, and a small text area to show whether the program is in plot or move mode, has fast or slow movement, will fill or line-draw shapes, and, finally, the colour in which it will plot. You will discover that, as in the last program, you cannot move the cursor off the screen, but if you choose B for box or O for circle, although the centre of the circle or bottom left corner must be within the border, the shape can extend out as far as you require.

This is one of my favourite programs for designing screen displays and it is possible to save the whole picture to tape using the *SAVE command when you have finished. If you prefer, you could do as I do and use it to design illustrations and dump them to a printer using a screen dump ROM.

Design

```
1000 REM   *** DESIGN ***
1010 REM
1020 REM   *** A.J.S. ***
1030
1040 MODE2
1050 *FX11,20
1060 *FX12,5
1070
1080 REM   *** INITIALISATION  ***
1090
1100 col=7
1110 flag=1
1120 draw=4
1130 speed=8
1140 PROC_frame
1150
1160 REM   ***        WINDOWS       ***
1170
1180 VDU28,0,31,19,28
1190 VDU24,8;132;1271;1019;
1200 VDU23;8202;0;0;0;
1210
1220 PROC_wave
1230 PROC_main
1240 STOP
1250
1260 DEFPROC_main
1270 REPEAT
1280    *FX15,0
1290    N%=GET
1300    PROC_decode
1310    PLOT70,X%,Y%
1320    FORPAUSE=1TO100
1330      NEXT
1340    PLOT70,X%,Y%
1350    UNTIL FALSE
1360 ENDPROC
1370
1380 DEFPROC_decode
1390 IF N%>47 AND N%<59 THENcol = N%-48
1400 GCOL0,col
1410 IF N% = 44 THEN speed=8
```

```
1420 IF N% = 46 THEN speed=32
1430 IF N%=65 THEN X%=X%-speed:
     PROC_draw
1440 IF N%=68 THEN X%=X%+speed:
     PROC_draw
1450 IF N%=88 THEN Y%=Y%-speed:
     PROC_draw
1460 IF N%=87 THEN Y%=Y%+speed:
     PROC_draw
1470 IF N%=69 THEN X%=X%+speed:
     Y%=Y%+speed:PROC_draw
1480 IF N%=90 THEN X%=X%-speed:
     Y%=Y%-speed:PROC_draw
1490 IF N%=81 THEN X%=X%-speed:
     Y%=Y%+speed:PROC_draw
1500 IF N%=67 THEN X%=X%+speed:
     Y%=Y%-speed:PROC_draw
1510 IFN%=66 THEN PROC_box
1520 IFN%=79 THEN PROC_circle
1530 IFN%=70 THEN flag=81
1540 IFN%=76 THEN flag=1
1550 IF N%=77 THEN draw=4
1560 IF N%=80 THEN draw=5
1570 IF N%=84 THEN PROC_text
1580 PROC_wave
1590 N%=0
1600 ENDPROC
1610
1620 DEFPROC_draw
1630 IF X%<8 X%=8
1640 IF X%>1264 X%=1264
1650 IF Y%<132 Y%=132
1660 IF Y%>1012 Y%=1012
1670 PLOTdraw,X%,Y%
1680 ENDPROC
1690
1700 DEFPROC_frame
1710 MOVE0,128:DRAW0,1020:DRAW1272,1020
1720 DRAW1272,128:DRAW0,128
1730 MOVE640,560:X%=640:Y%=560:
     PROC_draw
1740 ENDPROC
1750
1760 DEFPROC_box
```

```
1770 COLOUR8
1780 PRINTTAB(8,0)"BOX "
1790 IF col<>0 THEN COLOURcol
1800 INPUT"Enter length - "len
1810 INPUT"Enter width  - "wid
1820 PLOT1,len,0
1830 PLOTflag,0,wid
1840 PLOT1,-len,0
1850 PLOTflag,0,-wid
1860 CLS
1870 ENDPROC
1880
1890 DEFPROC_circle
1900 COLOUR9
1910 PRINTTAB(7,0)"CIRCLE"
1920 IF col<>0 THEN COLOURcol
1930 INPUT"Enter radius - "rad
1940 MOVE X%,rad+Y%
1950 FOR N = 0 TO 2.1*PI STEP .2
1960   XS%=SIN N*rad+X%
1970   YS%=COS N*rad+Y%
1980   IF flag=81 MOVEX%,Y%
1990   PLOT flag+4,XS%,YS%
2000   NEXT N
2010 CLS
2020 ENDPROC
2030
2040 DEFPROC_wave
2050 IF col<>0 THEN COLOURcol
2060 IF draw=5 THEN PRINTTAB(0,0)"PLOT"
2070 IF draw=4 THEN PRINTTAB(0,0)"MOVE"
2080 IF flag=1 THEN PRINTTAB(16,0)
     "LINE";
2090 IF flag=81 THEN PRINTTAB(16,0)
     "FILL";
2100 IF speed=8 THEN PRINTTAB(8,0)
     "SLOW"
2110 IF speed=32THEN PRINTTAB(8,0)
     "FAST"
2120 ENDPROC
2130
2140 DEFPROC_text
2150 PRINT"ENTER TEXT"
2160 INPUT text$
```

```
2170 VDU5
2180 PRINTtext$
2190 VDU4
2200 CLS
2210 ENDPROC
```

Notes on the program

Line 60 decreases slightly the amount of time before the auto-repeat starts. **Line 70** repeats at a rate of 20 characters a second, much faster than its normal rate.

Lines 110–140 initialise some variables: 'col' is the initial drawing colour; 'flag' is set to 1 for normal plotting; and 'speed' of plotting is set to 8.

Line 190 defines a text window. **Line 200** defines a graphics window.

PROC_main clears the input buffer, gets a key and sends it to PROC_decode for interpretation. **Lines 320** and **350** control the flashing cursor.

PROC_decode checks to see if certain keys have been pressed. If one of the keys chosen to move the cursor has been pressed, PROC_draw is selected.

Variable 'speed' controls how many pixels are drawn each time. The value can be either 8 for slow plotting, or 32 for fast plotting. If B is pressed, a box can be drawn. If O is pressed, a circle can be drawn. The < and > keys control the value of 'speed'. If F is pressed, the shapes are filled. If L is pressed, only the outline appears. If T is pressed, text can be entered at the position of the cursor on the screen.

PROC_draw keeps the drawing cursor on the screen. Although rectangles and circles can go outside the graphics window, the cursor must stay inside.

PROC_frame draws a line round the outside of the graphics window.

PROC_box draws a rectangle if the length and width are entered when requested. The colour of the text in the text window at the bottom of the screen is the same colour as the on-screen drawing colour, unless the colour is black. This is controlled in **line 800**.

PROC_circle uses sines and cosines to draw the circumference. This is one command that is missing from BBC BASIC, although it is not hard to implement. The variable 'flag' determines whether PLOT 5 for lines or PLOT 85 for filled in shapes should be used.

PROC_wave checks to see if the flags are waving, and prints messages in the text window so the user knows which mode they are in.

PROC_text uses VDU5 to print text at the graphics cursor. VDU4 is used to turn this effect off. The CLS will only clear the text window at the bottom of the screen and leave the graphics area untouched.

If you wish to erase the text window during the program, simply press <CTRL> and L. To clear the graphics area, press <CTRL> and P at the same time.

CHAPTER 4
Down to Business

Many people first come into contact with computers when they are encountered in some sort of business use. Such is the growth of micro-electronics that even small corner shops now use computers to check their accounts, write standard letters and to monitor their stock levels. Now that computing power is available at a reasonable price, it is possible to organise your home finances on a computer, and to check that your bank manager is handling your cash flow in the manner you expect.

Before you rush off madly putting all your financial affairs on to a computer, it is as well to carry out a feasibility study on the particular areas in which computerisation may prove useful.

Points in favour:
1) Calculations are fast.
2) You can receive a neat printout at the end.
3) It is easier to organise your money.
4) You can get fast graphs from the figures.

Points against:
1) It might take 10 minutes to set up the computer and load the program and the data.
2) The programs might not do all you want. This is often a problem with 'off-the-shelf' business software, and explains why there are so many computer consultancies in the country to customise the software.
3) You may not have enough transactions to make all the programming worthwhile.

If you decide that it is worthwhile putting everything on to your computer, the next stage is to decide what sort of software would be useful to you. Most business packages seem to fall into the standard areas of word-processing, database, spreadsheet, stock control and accounts.

Home accounts
The first program in this chapter is concerned with handling records of accounts. It stores records in three fields, although it would not be difficult to increase this number to accommodate extra information.

At present, you can enter the date, the amount and the subject. This is stored as one element in an array, and each field is partitioned by a different separator: a hash character and an asterisk, as these are unlikely to be used as characters in the fields.

If you need to store details of purchases through a financial year, this program will allow you to enter each transaction and to sort the entries into date order. If you need to total the amounts involved in separate categories, you can sort according to subject and you will be shown sub-totals. To achieve this, you will have to ensure that subject entries use an initial category such as STAT for stationery, etc. A typical entry for some printer paper bought at Smiths on the 31st July 1984 might be entered as:

310784
6.00
STAT PRINTER PAPER SMITHS

This would be encoded as:

840731#6.00*STAT PRINTER PAPER SMITHS

If you choose to sort according to date, the date entered has been reversed to allow this. If you wish to sort according to subject, the first field in each element in the array is removed by a procedure and tacked on the end, as explained in the notes, resulting in:

STAT PRINTER PAPER SMITHS#6.00*840731

The array can now be sorted according to subject.

You can use the same program to record income, as it will total amounts earned under different subjects as well as giving an overall total. This sort of program gives you a general idea of the types of procedures that could be incorporated in software tailor-made to your own specification. If you needed to record customers, amounts, dates, products and quantities, you would still use an array A$ to hold everything, but each record would be divided up into five fields separated by keys such as #, *, @ and &.

As in most of the programs in this book, the information is stored separately on a data file, thus making the program very flexible in use, and not so dependent on memory size.

```
          SEARCH DATABASE
      ENTER SEARCH STRING
?STAT PRESTEL

          15
Date=                      21/07/83
Amount=                       26.13
Subject=                   STAT PRESTEL

          31
Date=                      21/10/83
Amount=                       13.00
Subject=                   STAT PRESTEL

          51
Date=                      01/03/84
Amount=                       17.62
Subject=                   STAT PRESTEL

SUBTOTAL=          56.75

PRESS SPACE BAR TO CONTINUE
```

Figure 4.1: Screen Dump from Accounts.

Accounts

```
1000 REM   ***     ACCOUNTS      ***
1010 REM
1020 REM   ***  AJS 1/10/83   ***
1030
1040 MODE6
1050 PROC_init
1060 REPEAT
1070    PROC_menu
1080    UNTIL FALSE
1090
1100 DEFPROC_menu
1110 CLS
1120 PRINTTAB(15,2)"ACCOUNTS"
1130 PRINTTAB(5,5)"1 ADD NEW DATA"
1140 PRINTTAB(5,7)"2 DELETE DATA"
1150 PRINTTAB(5,9)"3 FIND DATA"
1160 PRINTTAB(5,11)"4 LIST DATA"
```

```
1170 PRINTTAB(5,13)"5 SORT DATA"
1180 PRINTTAB(5,15)"6 LOAD DATA"
1190 PRINTTAB(5,17)"7 SAVE DATA"
1200 PRINTTAB(5,19)"8 STOP PROGRAM"
1210 PRINTTAB(5,22)"PRESS A NUMBER"
1220 REPEAT
1230    Z=GET
1240    UNTIL Z>48 AND Z<57
1250 IF Z=49 THEN PROC_add
1260 IF Z=50 AND num%>0THEN PROC_change
1270 IF Z=51 AND num%>0 THEN PROC_find
1280 IF Z=52 AND num%>0 THEN PROC_list
1290 IF Z=53 AND num%>0 THEN
     PROC_sort(num%)
1300 IF Z=54 THEN PROC_load
1310 IF Z=55 THEN PROC_save
1320 IF Z=56 THEN STOP
1330 ENDPROC
1340
1350 DEFPROC_init
1360 VDU19,0,4;0;
1370 DIMA$(2000)
1380 num%=0
1390 VDU14
1400 ENDPROC
1410
1420 DEFPROC_add
1430 REPEAT
1440    num%=num%+1
1450    REPEAT
1460       CLS
1470       REPEAT
1480          PRINT"ENTER DATE ";
              "(8 Mar 84 is 080384)"
1490          INPUT date$
1500          date$=RIGHT$(date$,2)+
              MID$(date$,3,2)+
              LEFT$(date$,2)
1510          UNTIL LEN(date$)=6
1520       PRINT"ENTER AMOUNT ";
              "(`210.75 is 210.75)"
1530       INPUT amount$
1540       PRINT"ENTER THE SUBJECT"
1550       INPUTsubject$
```

```
1560       PRINT"IS THIS CORRECT?"
1570      Z$=GET$
1580       UNTIL Z$="Y"
1590    A$(num%)=date$+CHR$(35)+amount$
1600    A$(num%)=A$(num%)+CHR$(42)+
       subject$
1610    PRINTTAB(5,20)"PRESS SPACE BAR"
1620    PRINTTAB(10,21)"OR @ TO FINISH"
1630    UNTIL GET$="@"
1640 ENDPROC
1650
1660 DEFPROC_list
1670 total=0
1680 REPEAT
1690    CLS
1700    PRINT"PRESS S FOR SCREEN ";
       "OR P FOR PRINTER"
1710    Z$=GET$
1720    UNTIL Z$="S" OR Z$="P"
1730 CLS
1740 IF Z$="P" THEN VDU2:VDU15
1750 FOR N%=1 TO num%
1760    PROC_format(N%)
1770    NEXT
1780 PRINT ' "TOTAL = "total
1790 VDU3:VDU14
1800 PRINT
       "PRESS THE SPACE BAR TO CONTINUE"
1810 Z$=GET$
1820 ENDPROC
1830
1840 DEFPROC_sort(L%)
1850 flag=0
1860 CLS
1870 PRINTTAB(15,4)"SORT"
1880 PRINTTAB(5,8)
       "THE DATA MAY BE SORTED"
1890 PRINTTAB(5,9)
       "IN DATE ORDER, OR GROUPED"
1900 PRINTTAB(5,10)
       "ACCORDING TO SUBJECT"
1910 PRINTTAB(5,12)"CHOOSE 1 OR 2"
1920 PRINTTAB(5,14)"1 DATE"
1930 PRINTTAB(5,16)"2 SUBJECT"
```

```
1940 REPEAT
1950    Z=GET
1960     UNTIL Z=49 OR Z=50
1970 IFZ=50 THEN flag=1:PROC_swop
1980
1990 LOCALA%,B%,C%,D%,E$
2000 C%=(L%)DIV 2
2010   REPEAT
2020    FOR B%=1+C%TOL%
2030       FOR A%=B%-C%TO1 STEP -C%
2040         D%=A%+C%
2050          IF A$(A%)<=A$(D%) THEN 2100
2060          E$=A$(A%)
2070          A$(A%)=A$(D%)
2080          A$(D%)=E$
2090         NEXT A%
2100       NEXT B%
2110    C%=C% DIV2
2120     UNTIL C%=0
2130 IF flag = 1 THEN PROC_swop
2140 ENDPROC
2150
2160 DEFPROC_swop
2170 FOR N% = 1 TO num%
2180    P2=INSTR(A$(N%),CHR$(42))
2190    M$=MID$(A$(N%),P2+1)
2200    A$(N%)=M$+CHR$(42)+
       MID$(A$(N%),1,P2-1)
2210    NEXT N%
2220 ENDPROC
2230
2240 DEFPROC_find
2250 total=0:value=0
2260 REPEAT
2270    CLS
2280    PRINT"PRESS S FOR SCREEN ";
       "OR P FOR PRINTER"
2290    Z$=GET$
2300    UNTIL Z$="S" OR Z$="P"
2310 CLS
2320 PRINTTAB(12,3)"SEARCH DATABASE"
2330 PRINTTAB(5,5)"ENTER SEARCH STRING"
2340 IF Z$="P" THEN VDU2:VDU15
2350 INPUT search$
```

```
2360 FOR N% = 1 TO num%
2370    P2=INSTR(A$(N%),CHR$(42))
2380    compare$=
        MID$(A$(N%),P2+1,LEN(search$))
2390    IF compare$ = search$ THEN
        PROC_format(N%)
2400    NEXT N%
2410 @%=&02020A
2420 PRINT ' "SUBTOTAL= "total
2430 VDU3:VDU14
2440 @%=10
2450 PRINT
2460 PRINT"PRESS SPACE BAR TO CONTINUE"
2470 Z$=GET$
2480 ENDPROC
2490
2500 DEFPROC_format(N%)
2510 PRINT
2520 PRINTN%
2530 P1=INSTR(A$(N%),CHR$(35))
2540 P2=INSTR(A$(N%),CHR$(42))
2550 date$=LEFT$(A$(N%),P1-1)
2560 PRINT"Date= "
        TAB(20)RIGHT$(date$,2)"/";
2570 PRINT MID$(date$,3,2)"/"
        LEFT$(date$,2)
2580 @%=&02020A
2590 value=
        VAL(MID$(A$(N%),P1+1,P2-P1-1))
2600 total=total+value
2610 PRINT"Amount= "TAB(16)value
2620 @%=10
2630 subject$=
        RIGHT$(A$(N%),LEN(A$(N%))-P2)
2640 PRINT"Subject= "TAB(20)subject$
2650 ENDPROC
2660
2670 DEFPROC_save
2680 CLS
2690 INPUT ' "SAVING" '
        "ENTER A NAME-"file$
2700 x%=OPENOUT(file$)
2710 PRINT#x%,num%
2720 FOR N=1TOnum%
```

```
2730     PRINT#x%,A$(N)
2740     NEXT N
2750 CLOSE#x%
2760 CLS
2770 ENDPROC
2780
2790 DEFPROC_load
2800 CLS
2810 INPUT ' "LOADING" '
     "ENTER A NAME-"file$
2820 x%=OPENIN(file$)
2830 INPUT#x%,num%
2840 FOR N=1TOnum%
2850    INPUT#x%,A$(N)
2860     NEXT N
2870 CLOSE#x%
2880 CLS
2890 ENDPROC
2900
2910 DEFPROC_change
2920 CLS
2930 PRINTTAB(15,3)"CHANGE DATA"
2940 PRINTTAB(5,5)
     "ENTER THE RECORD NUMBER"
2950 REPEAT
2960    PRINTTAB(5,7)"       "
2970    INPUTTAB(5,7)record%
2980    UNTIL record% < num%+1
        AND record% >0
2990 PROC_format(record%)
3000 PRINT
3010 PRINT"ENTER D TO DELETE RECORD"
3020 PRINT"ANY OTHER KEY TO CONTINUE"
3030 Z$=GET$
3040 IF Z$="D" THEN PROC_delete
3050 IF Z$="D" THEN PRINT
     "RECORD DELETED"
3060 PRINT"PRESS SPACE BAR TO CONTINUE"
3070 Z$=GET$
3080 ENDPROC
3090
3100 DEFPROC_delete
3110 FOR N%=record% TO num%-1
3120    A$(N%)=A$(N%+1)
```

```
3130    NEXT N%
3140 num%=num%-1
3150 ENDPROC
```

Notes on the program

Line 1040 selects mode 6 to conserve memory. BBC users could save even more by using mode 7. **Lines 1040–1080** contain the control module.

PROC_menu lies between **lines 1100–1330**. This is fairly straightforward; it contains traps in **lines 1260–1290** to prevent users attempting to save or manipulate non-existent data.

PROC_init is contained in **lines 1350–1400**. **Line 1360** sets the background colour to blue. The array A$(n) holds all the information. In this program, each element (or record) of the array holds the date of the transaction, the amount (converted into a string), and the subject. The first two parts are separated by a hash character and the last two by an asterisk.

VDU14 turns page mode on. This is the same as <CTRL> N, and stops the display scrolling until <SHIFT> is pressed.

PROC_add allows information to be added to the array. **Lines 1480–1550** contain the date entry routine. The date is requested in a particular format: day, month and year. The numbers are reversed in **line 1500** so that the strings can be sorted in date order. The 15th of February, 1984 (840215), is considered to have a smaller value than the 20th of March, 1984 (840320).

Lines 1590 and **1600** stick the separate parts together, separated by CHR$(35), a hash sign, and CHR$(42), an asterisk.

PROC_list allows the user to look at all the entries in the order in which they were entered or in the order in which they appear after sorting.

Lines 1700–1740 and **line 1790** can be omitted if you are not using this with a printer. VDU2 switches the printer on and VDU3 switches it off. VDU15 switches off paged mode.

PROC_sort contains a binary sort routine that can sort on either the date or subject fields. This is achieved by **line 1970**. If the user has chosen to sort by dates, the array is sorted normally. The date field is the 'front-end' of each element, so will be sorted by date in any case. If the user chooses to sort by subject, then the program branches to PROC_swop, which moves the subject part of each element to the front, so that the sort takes place on this field first.

Local integer variables have been used to speed up the routine.

PROC_sort accepts the variable L% as a passed parameter: L% is the number of elements in the array, ie the number of entries in the file. This is necessary for the efficient operation of a binary sort, as the number is sliced in half for each pass of the routine.

Line 1970 sets a flag so that the elements may be returned to their former condition after the sort has taken place. This is achieved in **line 2130**.

PROC_swop is the routine to rearrange the elements if a subject sort is chosen. P2 is a variable that contains the position in the string of CHR$(42), the asterisk.

Line 2190 loads the first part of each element (ie the date) into M$, and **line 2200** tacks this section on to the end of the string, leaving the subject field at the front-end.

When PROC_swop is called again, the date field and subject field are swopped back to their rightful places.

PROC_find does a string search on each element using the very useful INSTR function. The search string only produces a result if it is found at the start of an element. This means that, if you have entered subjects using a code at the start, such as CAR REPAIRS, and CAR PETROL, then you can select all the entries to do with your motoring by entering the search string CAR. You will also get a sub-total of the amounts in this particular subgroup, which is a useful feature.

Line 2410 formats the amount neatly using the @% feature. Page 61 of the Electron guide or page 70 of the BBC guide explain this quite clearly. **Line 2440** sets the formatting back to normal.

PROC_format is used to pull each element of the array to pieces and present it on the screen in a meaningful fashion.

Line 2530 loads P1 with the position of the hash character, and **line 2540** loads P2 with the position of the asterisk. This allows the computer to know the start and finish of the three fields held in the element.

Lines 2560 and **2670** print the date in a normal manner separated by slashes.

Line 2580 sets the display of subsequent figures to a standard pounds and pence format. **Line 2590** prints the amount field of the string as a numeric value. **Line 2600** totals up the values of each element. Note that PROC_list and PROC_find set 'total' to 0 each time they are called.

PROC_save saves only the size of the array, and the array itself.

PROC_load, as usual, is very similar to PROC_save.

PROC_change allows the user to remove any information entered previously. **Line 2990** uses PROC_format to display the information present. If the entry is correct, there is the option to leave it as it is. **Line 3040** sends control to PROC_delete if the entry is incorrect.

PROC_delete moves all the records down one in memory to fill in the space occupied by the record that is not required.

The electronic diary

Another useful type of program in an office or in the home is an electronic diary. Ideally, this would be able to tell you your appointments for any particular day, whether that day was a Monday or a Wednesday, etc, and any other information you had entered into it. At this level, you would probably be no better off than if you had all this data in a pocket book.

To make it worthwhile as a piece of software, a diary program should exploit more of the features of the computer. It is possible to include a feature that will give you the day of the week for any date since 1752 but, more importantly, the program could search through the diary to find all references to computers, every meeting with your bank manager and in fact act like a tiny personal database.

The next program is designed to form a useful diary program that can store information on any date until the end of the century, but could be adapted to cover any dates you find necessary over the last 200 years. It will store a lot of entries but, should you run out of space, you could keep different subjects on separate files. Due to its adaptability, it could be used by several people in a home or an office, with everyone using separate data tapes.

There are several points that need to be mentioned. The first is the method used to find the days of the week. Our calendar stretches back to the days of Romulus. When he wasn't being suckled by wolves and founding cities with terrible traffic problems, he was apparently inventing a calendar containing 10 months. One of his successors, Numa Pompilius, brought the number of months up to 12. Julius Caesar improved upon this again and the Julian calendar, complete with leap years was used up until the sixteenth century. People began to notice that the seasons were getting a little out of step with the calendar and in 1582 Pope Gregory introduced the Gregorian calendar. This contained the extra idea that century years would only be leap years if they were also multiples of 400, ie 1900 wasn't, but 2000 will be. The Gregorian calendar was not introduced in Britain until 1752. For some years up to that date, it could be one year in Britain and the year after on the continent — very confusing.

It is not a simple matter to calculate any particular day, but there is a method that is suitable for computerisation that reduces the complexity somewhat. This is called Zeller's congruence, although you may find it attributed to the German mathematician Gauss in some books. It has the basic formula:

daynum =
INT(2.6*M−0.1) + day + Y + INT(Y/4) + INT(C/4)−2*C

where D is the day of the month, M is the month number starting with March and going on to February of the following year, Y is the value of the last pair of numbers in the year, and C the value of the first pair — so 4th August 1954 would be D = 4, M = 6, Y = 54 and C = 19. The answer is divided by 7 and the remainder is the number of the day of the week, starting with Sunday = 0. The exact formula has to be altered for some computers because of the way they handle remainders and rounding off.

When the diary program is run, the present date has to be entered and, after informing you of the particular day, a menu of options appears. These allow you to add data to the diary, to load or save information from a cassette or disk file, and to interrogate the program. This can be achieved in two ways: either by subject or by date. A date search simply turns to the page of the diary selected and displays any entries. A subject search goes through all the entries looking for any occurrence of the search string, even in the middle of an entry. If it is found, the whole of that 'page' is shown. Alternatively, you can choose to browse through all the entries.

The entries are stored in just one large array, entry$(n). At present it is dimensioned for 200 entries, but you could squeeze more in, provided they were short. The way the dates are held in the file is by coding them in a particular manner. Originally I wished to form a number by adding the date to 100 times the month number and 1000 times the value of the last two year numbers. This works well until you attempt to code months October, November and December, which of course have values of 1000, 1100 and 1200, which interferes with the year value.

```
84 times 1000 = 84000
11 times  100 =  1100
          20 =    20
code          = 85120
```

To get the details back from the code:

85120/1000 = 85 therefore year = 1985
The remainder is 120.
120/100 = 1 therefore month = Jan
The remainder is 20, so the date is the 20th.

Apparently, the date is now the 20th January 1985, not what was initially entered at all.

If the year is multiplied by 2000, and the month by 100, this does not occur.

```
84 times 2000 = 168000
11 times  100 =   1100
          20 =     20
code          = 169120
```

To get the details back from the code:

```
169120/2000 = 84 therefore year = 1984
The remainder is 1120.
1120/100 = 11, therefore month = Nov
The remainder is 20, so the date is the 20th.
```

I would be interested to know if any strange dates fail to work using this method!

The reason code numbers are given to the dates is so that the date code can be turned into a string using the STR$ function and then added to the beginning of each particular diary entry. It is separated from the actual entry by an asterisk, so that it can be identified in searches.

This method of storing information in the diary means that it can be entered in any order. The position of the entry in the diary does not matter as the program will search for any date you enter or for any string. The only irritation might be when you wish to browse through the entries if they are not in date order. To achieve this, there is another option available from the menu — sort. This is a binary sort that places the array elements in date order, because the date codes are at the start of each entry. It is probably a good idea to use this option after entering new information and before you save the file.

If you were interested in improving the program, you could add a delete routine similar to PROC_add or you might like a routine to print a calendar for the month in which you were interested. Those days with important entries could be shown in a different colour. However, as with many programs, this will reduce the number of items you can store in the diary, and you may prefer to use it as it is.

Diary

```
1000 REM   **      DIARY     **
1010 REM
1020 REM   ** AJS 1/2/84 **
1030
```

```
1040 MODE6
1050 PROC_init
1060 PROC_intro
1070 REPEAT
1080    PROC_menu
1090    UNTIL FALSE
1100
1110 DEFPROC_init
1120 VDU19,0,4;0;
1130 DIM entry$(200)
1140 number = 0
1150 flag=0
1160 ENDPROC
1170
1180 DEFPROC_intro
1190 PRINTTAB(15,1)"DIARY"
1200 PRINTTAB(0,3)STRING$(40,"*");
1210 PRINTTAB(5,5)
     "ENTER TODAY'S DATE"
1220 PRINTTAB(5,7)
     "USE THE NUMBER KEYS"
1230 PRINTTAB(5,9)"EG 12 4 1983"
1240 PROC_dateenter
1250 PROC_date(day%,month%,year%)
1260 PRINTTAB(5,18)"TODAY IS "day$
1270 PROC_daynum
1280 PRINTTAB(5,20)
     "AND ALSO DAY NUMBER "daynum%
1290 PRINTTAB(5,22)"PRESS SPACE BAR"
1300 Z$ = GET$
1310 ENDPROC
1320
1330 DEFPROC_dateenter
1340 REPEAT
1350    PRINTTAB(26,12)"       "
1360    INPUTTAB(5,12)
     "DAY (1 TO 31)        -"day%
1370    UNTIL day%>0 AND day%<32
1380 REPEAT
1390    PRINTTAB(26,14)"       "
1400    INPUTTAB(5,14)
     "MONTH (1 TO 12)      -"month%
1410    UNTIL month%>0 AND month%<13
1420 REPEAT
```

```
1430     PRINTTAB(26,16)"       "
1440     INPUTTAB(5,16)
         "YEAR (1983 TO 1999) -"year%
1450     UNTILyear%>1900 AND year%<2000
1460 ENDPROC
1470
1480 DEFPROC_menu
1490 CLS
1500 PRINTTAB(15,1)"DIARY"
1510 PRINTTAB(0,3)STRING$(40,"*");
1520 PRINTTAB(5,5)"1 ADD DETAILS"
1530 PRINTTAB(5,7)"2 FIND DATE"
1540 PRINTTAB(5,9)"3 FIND SUBJECT"
1550 PRINTTAB(5,11)"4 LOAD FILE"
1560 PRINTTAB(5,13)"5 SAVE FILE"
1570 PRINTTAB(5,15)"6 SORT FILE"
1580 PRINTTAB(5,17)"7 VIEW ALL ENTRIES"
1590 PRINTTAB(5,19)"8 STOP"
1600 PRINTTAB(5,22)"CHOOSE NUMBER"
1610 REPEAT
1620    Z=GET
1630    UNTIL Z>48 AND Z<57
1640 IF Z = 49 THEN PROC_add
1650 IF Z = 50 AND flag=1 THEN
     PROC_finddate
1660 IF Z = 51 AND flag=1 THEN
     PROC_subject
1670 IF Z = 52 THEN PROC_load
1680 IF Z = 53 AND flag=1 THEN
     PROC_save
1690 IF Z = 54 AND flag=1 THEN
     PROC_sort
1700 IF Z = 55 AND flag=1 THEN
     PROC_view
1710 IF Z = 56 THEN STOP
1720 ENDPROC
1730
1740 DEFPROC_date(day%,month%,year%)
1750 month%=month%-2
1760 IF month%<1 THEN month%=month%+12:
     year%=year%-1
1770 year$ = STR$(year%)
1780 century% = INT(year%/100)
1790 endyr% = VAL(RIGHT$(year$,2))
```

```
1800 A% = INT(2.6*month%-0.19)+day%+
     endyr%+INT(endyr%/4)+
     INT(century%/4)-century%*2
1810 wkday%=A%MOD7
1820 wkday%=wkday%+1
1830 RESTORE 3270
1840 FOR N%=1TO wkday%
1850    READ day$
1860    NEXT N%
1870 ENDPROC
1880
1890 DEFPROC_daynum
1900 LOCAL total%
1910 RESTORE 3310
1920 total%=0
1930 FOR N%=1 TO month%
1940    READ monthdays%
1950    total%=total%+monthdays%
1960    NEXT N%
1970 daynum%=total%+day%
1980 IF year%MOD4=0 AND month%>2 THEN
     daynum%=daynum%+1
1990 ENDPROC
2000
2010 DEFPROC_finddate
2020 CLS
2030 PRINTTAB(15,2)"FIND DATE"
2040 PRINTTAB(0,4)STRING$(40,"*");
2050 PRINTTAB(0,6)"ENTER THE DATE"
2060 PROC_dateenter
2070 code% = (year%-1900)*2000+month%*
     100+day%
2080 found = 0
2090 date$=STR$(code%)
2100 FOR X = 1 TO number
2110    IF LEN(date$)>LEN(entry$(X))
       THEN2140
2120    found=INSTR(entry$(X),date$)
2130    IF found<>0 THEN PROC_display
2140    NEXT X
2150 ENDPROC
2160
2170 DEFPROC_add
2180 number = number+1
```

```
2190 CLS
2200 PRINTTAB(12,2)"ADD INFORMATION"
2210 PRINTTAB(0,4)STRING$(40,"*");
2220 PROC_dateenter
2230 PROC_daynum
2240 VDU28,0,24,39,6
2250 COLOUR130
2260 CLS
2270 REPEAT
2280    PRINT"ENTER THE DETAILS"
2290    PRINT"(NOT MORE THAN 6 LINES)"
2300    INPUT detail$
2310    code% = (year%-1900)*2000+
        month%*100+day%
2320    entry$(number) = STR$(code%)+
        "*"+detail$
2330    PRINT"IS THIS CORRECT?"
2340    Z$ = GET$
2350    UNTIL Z$ = "Y" OR Z$ = "y"
2360 VDU26
2370 flag=1
2380 ENDPROC
2390
2400 DEFPROC_subject
2410 CLS
2420 PRINTTAB(12,2)"FIND INFORMATION"
2430 PRINTTAB(0,4)STRING$(40,"*");
2440 PRINTTAB(0,6)
     "ENTER THE SEARCH STRING"
2450 INPUT search$
2460 found = 0
2470 FOR X = 1 TO number
2480    IF LEN(search$)>LEN(entry$(X))
        THEN 2510
2490    found=INSTR(entry$(X),search$)
2500    IF found<>0 THEN PROC_display
2510    NEXT X
2520 ENDPROC
2530
2540 DEFPROC_display
2550 pos=INSTR(entry$(X),"*")
2560 date$=LEFT$(entry$(X),pos)
2570 date%=VAL(date$)
2580 year% = 1900 + (date%/2000)
```

```
2590 month%= (date% MOD 2000)/100
2600 day%  = (date% MOD 2000) MOD 100
2610 PROC_date(day%,month%,year%)
2620 CLS
2630 PRINTTAB(2,2)"Date:- ";day%;
     " Month%:- ";month%;" Year:- ";
     year%
2640 PRINTTAB(2,4)day$
2650 PRINT
2660 PRINTTAB(0,6)MID$(entry$(X),pos)
2670 PRINT
2680 PRINT"PRESS SPACE BAR"
2690 Z$ = GET$
2700 ENDPROC
2710
2720 DEFPROC_save
2730 CLS
2740 PRINTTAB(14,1)"SAVING FILE"
2750 PRINTTAB(0,3)STRING$(40,"*")
2760 INPUTTAB(0,6)"ENTER A NAME- "file$
2770 x%=OPENOUT(file$)
2780 PRINT#x%,number
2790 FOR X = 1 TO number
2800    PRINT#x%,entry$(X)
2810    NEXT X
2820 CLOSE#x%
2830 ENDPROC
2840
2850 DEFPROC_load
2860 CLS
2870 PRINTTAB(14,1)"LOADING FILE"
2880 PRINTTAB(0,3)STRING$(40,"*")
2890 INPUTTAB(0,6)"ENTER NAME - "file$
2900 x%=OPENIN(file$)
2910 INPUT#x%,number
2920 FOR X = 1 TO number
2930    INPUT#x%,entry$(X)
2940    NEXT X
2950 CLOSE#x%
2960 flag=1
2970 ENDPROC
2980
2990 DEFPROC_view
3000 CLS
```

```
3010 PRINTTAB(12,1)"VIEW ALL ENTRIES"
3020 PRINTTAB(0,3)STRING$(40,"*")
3030 VDU28,0,24,39,6
3040 FOR X = 1 TO number
3050    PROC_display
3060    NEXT X
3070 VDU26
3080 ENDPROC
3090
3100 DEFPROC_sort
3110 LOCALA%,B%,C%,D%,E$
3120 C% = number DIV 2
3130 REPEAT
3140    FOR B%=1+C% TO number
3150       FOR A%=B%-C% TO 1 STEP -C%
3160          D% = A% + C%
3170          IF entry$(A%)<=entry$(D%)
             THEN 3220
3180          E$ = entry$(A%)
3190          entry$(A%) = entry$(D%)
3200          entry$(D%) = E$
3210          NEXT A%
3220       NEXT B%
3230    C%=C% DIV2
3240    UNTIL C%=0
3250 ENDPROC
3260
3270 DATA SUNDAY,MONDAY,TUESDAY
3280 DATA WEDNESDAY,THURSDAY,FRIDAY
3290 DATA SATURDAY
3300
3310 DATA 0,31,28,31,30,31,30,31,31,30
3320 DATA 31,30
```

Notes on the program

PROC_init sets the background colour to blue, reserves space for 200 entries, and sets the variable 'flag' to 0 to show there is no data in the memory yet.

PROC_intro allows the user to enter the initial date and it also calculates the number of days into the year.

PROC_dateenter is a procedure that error-traps the input to a certain degree. It will not allow the user to enter a date less than 1 or greater than 31, a month less than 1 or greater than 12, and a year less than 1983 and greater than 2000. The last set of values can be changed if you want to record events outside these limits.

PROC_menu gives the standard menu of choices. There are eight options, including saving and loading files, entering dates, finding one particular date, finding occurrences of a subject, viewing all the records and sorting. Note the use of the variable 'flag' to inhibit the use of all the options except loading and entering when there is no information in memory.

PROC_date contains Zeller's formula to calculate the day of the week. When it is called from another part of the program, the procedure name has to be followed by three parameters, the day, month and year, which are used in the calculation.

Line **1830** restores the data pointer so that the names of the days can be read from the data lines. Line **1810** uses the function MOD to give the remainder when the answer is divided by 7.

PROC_daynum adds up the days in each month to the present date. Line **1910** restores the data pointer to the start of the data lines that contain the number of days in each month.

Line **1980** adds on a day for leap years. Note that this would need to be altered if years such as 1900 were included.

PROC_finddate searches through the whole array for the date. Due to the method employed here, if the date has more than one entry, that will also be found, which could be useful.

Line **2070** codes the date as explained before, and line **2090** turns it into a string.

Line **2110** is an escape line for anyone using this program on some early BBC machines which contain the INSTR bug. If the search string is larger than the string with which it is being compared, a nasty crash happens.

Lines **2100–2150** contain the loop that checks through each entry. If the string is found, the variable 'found' no longer has the value 0 and control jumps to PROC_display.

PROC_add is used to make new entries in the diary. Line **2240** defines a text window for the entry. Lines **2310** and **2320** code the date as explained before. Line **2360** returns the text window to its normal full screen size. Line **2370** sets variable 'flag' to 1 to show that there is information in the memory.

PROC_subject is very similar to PROC_finddate and is used to search through the database for occurrences of the search string.

PROC_decode slices off the date section of the entry string in **line 2560** and turns it into a numeric variable. The details of the date and the day of the week are printed out across the top of the screen, and the rest of the diary entry appears beneath in **line 2660**.

Variable 'pos' is used to point out the position of the separating asterisk in the string.

PROC_save and **PROC_load** are, if anything, simpler than that used in most programs. They simply save the number of entries and the array, entry$(n).

PROC_view goes through all the entries and displays them one at a time.

PROC_sort is a binary sort as used in several other programs.

At the end of the program are found the data lines providing the days of the week and length of the months.

Graphs and charts

The way information is displayed can often make an important difference to how the results are interpreted. A column of figures or a table of results is often meaningless until a picture is drawn. The picture itself can take on a variety of forms — from an early age at school, children are encouraged to show their results in the form of bar charts and block graphs. At a simple level, this may amount to little more than cut-out pictures of cars and lorries as part of a traffic survey. Later on, real objects are represented first by blocks and then by straight lines.

It is not only children who understand better when information is presented pictorially. Most business software packages contain a graphics program to present multi-coloured pictures of how well company salespersons are performing. At election time, pie charts are used to show the slices of the electorate that have been gobbled up by the parties. Advertisements often show (misleadingly) how good products are for you.

To complete this chapter on business programs, I have included a graph production program. At the start you are shown a menu with a choice of two types of display: either a pie chart or a block graph can be drawn. The pie chart is limited in the number of possible categories that may be shown, but is often clearer for 'share-out' types of information. The block graph section will show clearly a dozen or so categories, eg for

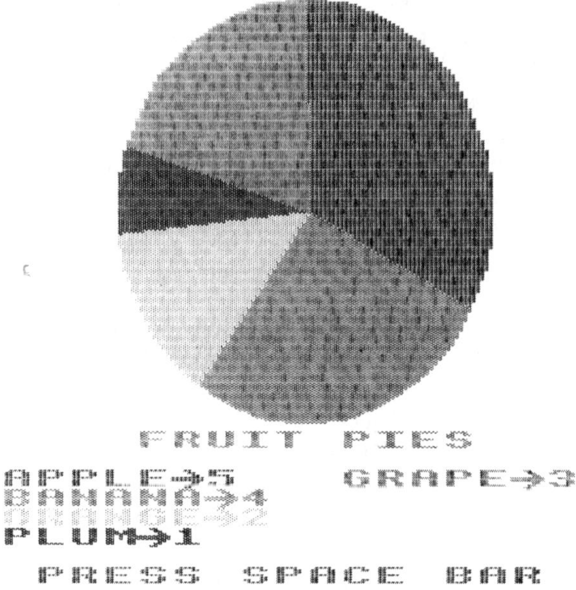

Figure 4.2: Screen Dump from Unigraph – Pie Chart.

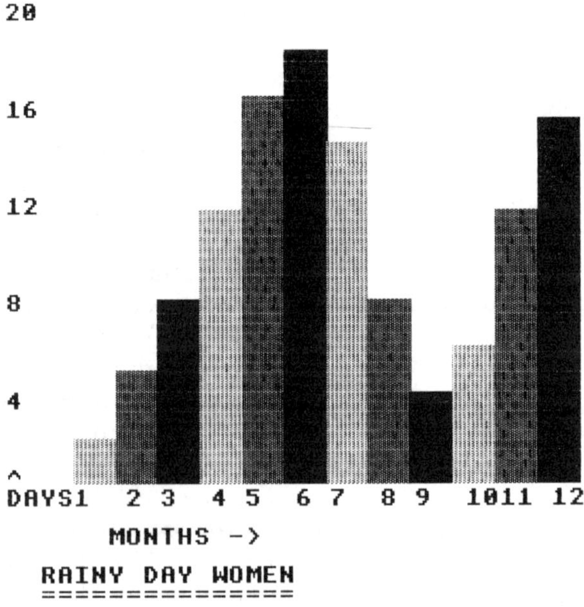

Figure 4.3: Screen Dump from Unigraph – Block Graph.

months in a year, but, as the program includes an automatic column numbering routine, it may look confusing above this number. If you want to display regular large numbers, then you will either have to change the mode to zero and lose the variety of colours or, more simply, remove the numbering routine entirely.

The first information requested is the number of subject categories. The maximum number in any one category is needed next. Before the data in each category is entered, there are prompts for the axis labels. Lastly, a title is requested, the numbers in each group are entered and the chart appears on the screen.

There is more than one way in which blocks of colour can be drawn on the screens of Acorn computers. A fairly obvious way would be to use the PLOT 85,X,Y statement. This fills in a triangle between the X,Y position and the last two points plotted. This technique has been used in the graphics chapter in this book to draw rectangles, but it is by no means the fastest way of colouring in boxes on the screen.

Both the BBC micro and the Electron allow the user to define windows on the display, where either graphics or text can appear. If a graphics window is defined and then cleared, the current background colour fills the window. It was decided to use this method both for its speed, and for its simplicity in programming.

From the initial information, the program calculates the size of each graphics window in terms of position and width. The base is fixed on the X axis, and the height depends on the number in a particular category and the scaling factor. Each window is drawn by a procedure that uses parameters calculated in the main program.

To make it easier to use, the program numbers the Y axis automatically (this routine is better if the maximum chosen is at least six).

Unigraph

```
1000 REM   ***          UNIGRAPH          ***
1010
1020 REM   ***   AJS/PH   10/10/83   ***
1030
1040 PROC_graphics
1050 PROC_init
1060
1070 REPEAT
1080    MODE2
1090    PROC_explain
1100    IFZ$="1"THEN PROC_pie:GOTO 1160
1110    MODE6
```

```
1120    PROC_title
1130    PROC_inputblock
1140    MODE1
1150    PROC_graph
1160    UNTIL FALSE
1170
1180 DEFPROC_graphics
1190 VDU 23, 224, &0, &0, &0, &FF, &FF,
     &FF, &0, &0
1200 VDU 23, 225, &18, &C, &6, &FF,&FF,
     &6, &C, &18
1210 ENDPROC
1220
1230 DEF PROC_init
1240 DIM it$( 7 )
1250 DIM value( 7 )
1260 DIM angle( 7 )
1270 A$ = "PRESS SPACE BAR"
1280 ENDPROC
1290
1300 DEFPROC_explain
1310 VDU 19, 0, 7, 0, 0, 0
1320 COLOUR 1
1330 PRINTTAB(5,4)"UNIGRAPH"
1340 FOR N = 5 TO 12
1350    VDU31,N,5,224
1360    NEXT N
1370 COLOUR4
1380 PRINTTAB(2,9)"PRESS THE NUMBER"
1390 PRINTTAB(2,11)"OF YOUR CHOICE"
1400 PRINTTAB(2,14)"1 PIE CHART"
1410 PRINTTAB(2,16)"2 BLOCK GRAPH"
1420 REPEAT
1430    Z$=GET$
1440    UNTIL Z$ = "1" OR Z$ = "2"
1450 ENDPROC
1460
1470 DEFPROC_pie
1480 CLS
1490 PRINTTAB(0,2)" YOU MUST TYPE :-"
1500 PRINTTAB(0,4)" 1. THE TITLE"
1510 COLOUR 1
1520 PRINTTAB(0,6)"( 15 LETTERS MAX)"
1530 COLOUR 4
```

```
1540 PRINTTAB(0,10)" 2. NO. OF ITEMS"
1550 COLOUR 1
1560 PRINTTAB(0,12)"( MAX OF 7 )"
1570 COLOUR 4
1580 PRINTTAB(0,16)" 3. VAL. FOR EACH"
1590 COLOUR 1
1600 PRINTTAB(0,18)"( NO LIMIT )"
1610 PRINT TAB(2,25)A$
1620 VDU 30 : * FX 15, 0
1630 REPEAT : K = GET : UNTIL K = 32
1640 PROC_inputpie
1650 PROC_chart
1660 ENDPROC
1670
1680 DEFPROC_inputpie
1690 CLS
1700 PRINTTAB(2,2)"ENTER YOUR DATA"
1710 COLOUR 4
1720 REPEAT
1730    PRINTTAB(1,5)SPC(40)
1740    INPUTTAB(1,5)"TITLE "title$
1750    UNTIL LENtitle$<21ANDLENtitle$>0
1760 REPEAT
1770    PRINTTAB(1,7)SPC(40)
1780    INPUTTAB(1,7)"NO. OF ITEMS? "num
1790    UNTIL num<8 AND num>0
1800 FOR N = 1 TO num
1810    COLOUR 1
1820    PRINTTAB(1,3*N+6)"ITEM";N
1830    COLOUR 4
1840    REPEAT
1850       PRINTTAB(1,3*N+7)SPC(40)
1860       INPUTTAB(1,3*N+7)"NAME "it$(N)
1870       len=LEN it$(N)
1880       UNTIL len<14 AND len>0
1890    COLOUR 2
1900    REPEAT
1910       ps=3*N+8
1920       PRINTTAB(1,ps)SPC(40)
1930       INPUTTAB(1,ps)"VALUE "value(N)
1940       UNTIL value(N)>0
1950    NEXT N
1960 ENDPROC
1970
```

```
1980 DEFPROC_chart
1990 CLS
2000 VDU 19, 0, 7, 0, 0, 0
2010 VDU 19, 7, 0, 0, 0, 0
2020 sum = 0 : start = 0
2030 FOR N = 1 TO num
2040    sum = sum + value(N)
2050    NEXT N
2060 FOR N = 1 TO num
2070    angle(N) = 2 * PI * value(N)/sum
2080    NEXT N
2090 MOVE640,1000
2100 FOR N=1 TO num
2110    GCOL 0, N
2120    finish = start + angle(N)
2130    FOR J=start TO finish STEP PI/60
2140      MOVE 640, 650
2150      PLOT 85, 640 + 350 * SIN( J ),
          650 + 350 * COS(J)
2160      NEXT J
2170    start = start + angle(N)
2180    NEXT N
2190 PRINTTAB((20-LEN title$)/2,23)
     title$
2200 FOR N=1 TO num
2210    COLOUR N
2220    IF N<5 THEN X = 1:Y = 24 + N
        ELSE X = 11:Y = 20+N
2230    IFN<num-3 THEN L = 7 ELSE L =13
2240    IF N > 4 THEN L = 7
2250    PRINTTAB(X,Y)LEFT$(it$(N),L-LEN
        STR$ value(N))CHR$ 225;value(N)
2260    NEXT N
2270 COLOUR 1
2280 PRINTTAB(2,30)A$
2290 VDU 30:*FX 15,0
2300 REPEAT:K = GET:UNTIL K = 32
2310 ENDPROC
2320
2330 PROC_inputblock
2340 DEFPROC_graph
2350 FOR N = 0 TO 25 STEP 5
2360    yaxis=INT(0.1+max/25*N)
2370    PRINTTAB(0,26-N);yaxis
```

```
2380     NEXT N
2390  FOR N = 1 TO catnum
2400     PRINTTAB(2+30/catnum*N,26);N
2410     NEXT N
2420  FOR N=0 TO catnum-1
2430     a=N*(950/catnum)+950/catnum+50
2440     c=N*(950/catnum)+1900/catnum+50
2450     d=cat(N)+200
2460     e=129+N MOD 3
2470     PROC_draw(a,c,d,e)
2480     NEXT N
2490  PRINTTAB(2,30)graphtitle$
2500  FOR N = 1 TO LEN graphtitle$
2510     PRINTTAB(1+N,31)"=";
2520     NEXT N
2530  PRINTTAB(6,28)cattitle$;" ->"
2540  PRINTTAB(0,25)"^"
2550  PRINTTAB(0,26)ytitle$
2560  VDU5
2570  Z$=GET$
2580  ENDPROC
2590
2600  DEFPROC_draw(a,c,d,e)
2610  GCOL 0,e
2620  VDU24,a;200;c;d;
2630  CLG
2640  ENDPROC
2650
2660  DEFPROC_title
2670  INPUT"Enter no. of categories "
      catnum
2680  PRINT"Enter a title for the ";
      "categories"
2690  INPUT cattitle$
2700  INPUT"Enter largest value "max
2710  PRINT"Enter a short title for ";
      "the Y values"
2720  INPUT"(less than 6 chrs.) "ytitle$
2730  DIM cat(catnum)
2740  PRINT"Enter a title for the graph"
2750  INPUT graphtitle$
2760  PRINT"Enter no. in each category"
2770  ENDPROC
2780
```

```
2790 DEFPROC_inputblock
2800 FOR N=0 TO catnum-1
2810    PRINT"CATEGORY ";N+1;
2820    REPEAT
2830       INPUTcat(N)
2840       UNTIL cat(N)>=0 AND cat(N)
          <=max
2850    cat(N)=cat(N)/max*750
2860    NEXT
2870 ENDPROC
```

Notes on the program

Lines 1070–1160 contain the control module.

PROC_graphics defines characters 224 and 225.

PROC_init dimensions space for various arrays and the string A$.

PROC_explain contains the instructions and sets the colour. **Line 1360** uses VDU31, which is another way of saying PRINT AT.

PROC_pie gives the user information on how to enter data for the pie chart. **Line 1630** homes the text cursor and clears the input buffer.

PROC_inputpie allows the data to be entered.

PROC_chart uses sines and cosines to draw a circle and PLOT 85 to fill it in. Both graphs wait for a key to be pressed at the end of their respective plotting routines, although there is no screen prompt to indicate this as it was thought this might detract from the display.

PROC_graph draws the graph according to the information entered in PROC_title and PROC_inputblock. The rather strange values are simply those found to position the graph best on the screen.

Notice the routine in **lines 2430–2490**. This calculates the values of a, c and d which determine the size and position of the windows in PROC_draw, and uses MOD3 to calculate the colour of the window. If this program was rewritten in mode 2, you could have seven alternate colours by using MOD7.

PROC_draw(a,c,d,e) accepts four parameters necessary to draw the windows. Parameter e controls the colour, and a, c and d the position of the window.

PROC_title merely suggests maximum lengths for titles, etc, and could be error-trapped if desired.

PROC_inputblock is the routine to accept data in each category.

CHAPTER 5
The Crystal Ball

Statistics

It was Mark Twain who said, 'There are lies, damned lies, and statistics'. This is the sort of remark that comes to mind at certain times of the year, particularly when there is an election about to take place, or when some sort of official body is about to make some drastic changes: 'According to recently published statistics from the Ministry of . . .' is a phrase to encourage support for Mr Twain's views. In fact, we use elementary statistics all the time in our daily lives and think nothing of it. It is the misuse, and not the use, of statistics that should worry us.

Many people use budget accounts to make expenditure slightly less painful; these take your total annual expenditure and share out the repayments equally between each month. Insurance firms divide the cost of claim payments between all policy-holders to arrive at an average premium (after including their profits, naturally enough!). Without our acceptance of useful statistics, living in the twentieth century would be less easy.

If, however, a bus company says that according to a statistical survey, only 30 people use a village service each week and so the service must be cut as a non-viable proposition, then this might turn some people against statistics. This feeling is certainly justified if 25 people use the bus once a week on Thursdays to go to the market and the survey has ignored this fact. Statistics provide a tool, but as in all cases they can wreak havoc if handled unwisely.

The word 'mean' in statistics is what most people understand by average. If your team scores three goals in one match, then four, one, and nil in subsequent games, the total scored is eight in four matches. The mean score is two, as $8/4 = 2$. It does not matter that no match actually has a result of two. It's similar to a situation where four people put money into a pool and then share it out. It's possible that none of the four will actually end up with the same amount that they put in.

Graphs are useful ways to look at any collection of data. They tend to show immediately if there is any pattern in the information that has been collected. Sometimes data values increase uniformly, ie 1, 2, 3, 4, 5 or 1, 4, 7, 10, etc. If these sets of data were plotted upon a regular time scale, they would produce a straight line, sloping upwards. If the values were 1,

4, 9, 16, etc, the graph would not form a straight line, but it would still be possible to plot the points on a smooth curve.

Sometimes the results would form a different shape again. One common expression is 'normal distribution'. Many human attributes are normally distributed, eg height, weight, intelligence, running speed, size of feet, etc. If you looked at heights, for instance, you would find very few adults less than 4 ft; there would be considerably more between 4 ft and 5 ft; an awful lot between 5 ft and 6 ft; fewer between 6 ft and 7 ft; and hardly any who were taller than 7 ft. A survey of heights would show a hill-like graph, showing that most people are in the middle, with average heights, tailing away on both sides to hardly any very short and very tall people. You can see that a graph of weights or of intelligence would also produce a similar shape. This shape is called a normal distribution curve.

If you carry out a statistical survey, it is useful to see if your results are normally distributed. If they are, they will not vary much from the mean of your results. Look at these two sets of data:

a) 1,4,5,6,8,12
b) 5,5,6,6,7,7

They both add up to 36, so they both have a mean of 6. It's clear that the values are spread out in different ways. Finding how the values are distributed in each sample will give a standard way of describing the differences. Those in (b) are clustered round the value 6, whereas those in (a) vary quite a lot from the mean.

The usual statistical technique is to calculate by how much each score deviates from the mean. This is done by:

a) Subtracting the mean from each score.
b) Squaring these deviations.
c) Totalling these results.
d) Sharing these by the number of scores, less one.

This result is called the variance, and the square root of this is called the standard deviation. A small result implies a higher consistency in the data. (Unfortunately, government departments don't usually publish the means and standard deviations of their surveys, so you can't determine how much weight could be attached to them.)

Expressed as a formula, this can be written as:

$$S = \sqrt{\frac{\Sigma(x - <x>)^2}{N-1}}$$

where x   = each individual score
   <x> = mean score
   N   = total number of scores
   Σ = 'the sum of'
   SQR = 'the square root of'
   S   = standard deviation

Sometimes you may see this formula with N underneath rather than N−1. With large sample numbers the difference between the two results is likely to be very small.

The variance of the values in (a) is 14, and the standard deviation 3.74. The variance of (b) is 0.8 and the standard deviation 0.89. To save your poor brain all that calculation, here is the BASIC equivalent of the SD formula.

Elementary Stats

```
1000 REM **   Elementary stats  **
1010 REM
1020 REM **      AJS 1/11/83     **
1030
1040 REM **       Initialise     **
1050
1060 DIM number(100)
1070 MODE 1
1080 COLOUR129
1090 CLS
1100 X = 0
1110 sum = 0
1120 var = 0
1130
1140 REM **      Data entry      **
1150
1160 PRINTTAB(14,2)"STATISTICS"
1170 PRINTTAB(0,3)STRING$(40,"*")
1180 PRINTTAB(11,5)"Enter your data"
1190 PRINTTAB(7,7)
     "Press [RETURN] to stop"
1200 PRINT
1210 X=X+1
1220 PRINT X;") ";
1230 INPUT number$
1240 IF number$ = "" THEN 1290
```

```
1250 number(X) = VAL(number$)
1260 sum = sum + number(X)
1270 mean = sum/X
1280 GOTO 1210
1290 X=X-1
1300
1310 REM  **        Calculate       **
1320
1330 FOR N=1 TO X
1340    diff = number(N)-mean
1350    var = var + (diff*diff/(X-1))
1360    NEXT N
1370 deviation = SQR(var)
1380
1390 REM  **        Display        **
1400
1410 PRINT
1420 PRINTTAB(2)
     "Size of sample = ";X
1430 PRINTTAB(2)
     "Sum of numbers = ";sum
1440 PRINTTAB(2)
     "Mean           = ";mean
1450 PRINTTAB(2)
     "Variance       = ";var
1460 PRINTTAB(2)
     "Deviation      = ";deviation
```

Chances and probability

The previous program shows how the computer can bring some order to a pile of assorted data by calculating the variance and the standard deviation. Can we develop this ability to look into the future?

Predicting the future seems more like a fun activity at the fair than a serious subject for a computer program. In fact, in many cases it is possible to make a reasonable guess at what is likely to take place if an existing trend carries on into the future. This is what most statistical operations are based on: knowledge of past and present conditions being used to predict future events.

If you spin a coin in the air, there is a 50:50 chance it will land on a head, and the same likelihood it will hand on a tail (I'm ignoring the tiny, but real, possibility of it landing on its edge). If you have already spun it 99 times and these were all tails, the next spin still only has a 50:50 chance of being a head, so you stand no greater chance of predicting the outcome than you had at the first spin. However, such a result might make you suspicious about the true nature of the coin. This might have two tails, although there *is* a possibility that the result has occurred by pure chance. Gambling against this possibility gives us the opportunity to say, not what is bound to happen, but what is likely to happen.

If you are the manager of a toy-shop and you sold one teddybear the first week, two the next and three the week after that, you might reasonably assume that you would sell four during the following week.

If you drew a graph of sales against time, it would be a straight line rising upwards. If you sold four kites the first week, three the next and two the week after that, you would probably predict that sales were falling in a regular fashion, and you would probably only sell one during the next week. A graph of your progress would show a slope downwards, but still in a straight line.

Supposing your sales of skipping ropes were five in the first week, four in the week after, six after that, then seven, the pattern would be more complicated, but it would still be possible to discern an upward trend. A line drawn between the points would no longer be straight, due to the hiccup in week 2. In spite of this, you could still draw a line that passed close to most of the points. This is called a 'line of best fit', and need not in fact, pass through any of the points.

A problem arises when you have several values that are not on the line. Is it fair to draw a straight line graph? If the figures bounce all over the place in a random fashion, then clearly it is not. What we need is some means of telling if the points are reasonably close to the line. If they are, then we can continue the line of best fit into the future, and make a prediction about the sales.

How well a line fits the given data is known as the coefficient of linear regression, and there is a fairly hefty formula to calculate this. With a computer, it is a comparatively easy job to calculate the line of best fit from data and therefore also to find the coefficient. If the data fits the line exactly, the coefficient has a value of 1, although the expressed variance is usually shown as a percentage, with 100% being the same as a coefficient of 1.

The following program accepts data entered along a regular timescale, in this case months. The more data entered, the more accurate the result is likely to be. When you have entered all the points you can, the computer calculates the line of best fit, and what the variation, V, is each month. Tracing the line back will give the graph an imaginary starting value in month 0, Z.

The formula $Y = Z * X + V$ gives the value Y for month number X. It also shows whether your data can be considered to fit on a straight line. How well it fits (the variance) is also shown as a percentage — 100% means the points are all along the line, 0% means your data certainly isn't linear!

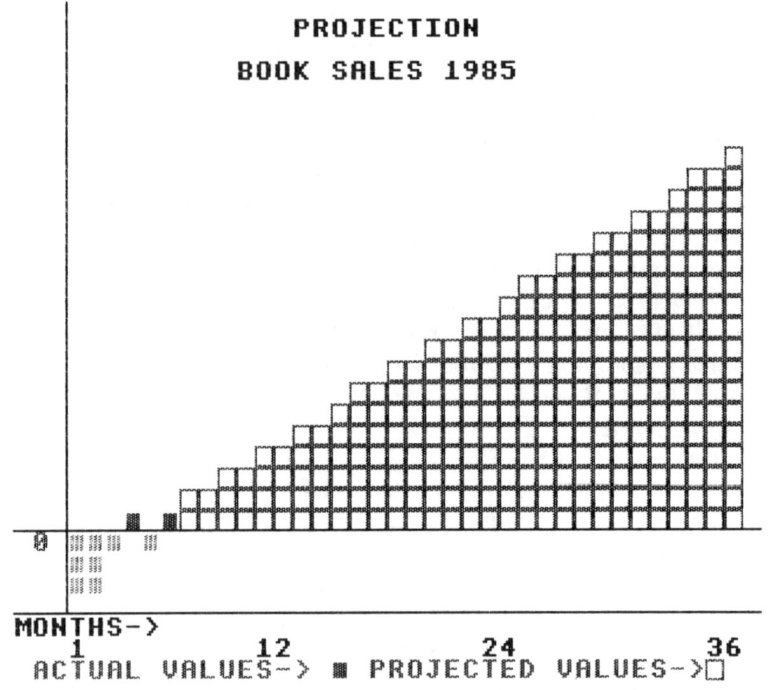

Figure 5.1: Screen Dump from Linear Projections.

Provided the timescale is linear, you could substitute any time increments along the bottom instead of months. It should be clear that linear regression technique only works, naturally enough, for growth or shrinkage that can fit on a straight line. The program can't predict non-linear progressions, and will attempt to flatten out nice sequences like squares (1,4,9,16,25, etc) or Fibonacci (1,1,2,3,5,8,13,21, etc). This means that you won't be very accurate if you try to forecast how many rabbits you'll have in your hutch this time next year.

Linear Projections

```
1000 REM   ***   LINEAR PROJECTIONS   ***
1010 REM
1020 REM   ***     AJS   20/10/83     ***
1030
1040 MODE1
1050 VDU19,3,2;0;
1060 PROC_init
```

```
1070 REPEAT
1080    PROC_menu
1090    UNTIL FALSE
1100
1110 DEFPROC_menu
1120 CLS
1130 PRINTTAB(15,1)"FORECAST"
1140 PRINTTAB(0,3)STRING$(40,"*")
1150 PRINTTAB(9,8)"1 ENTER DATA"
1160 PRINTTAB(9,11)"2 PRODUCE FORECAST"
1170 PRINTTAB(9,14)"3 DISPLAY DATA"
1180 PRINTTAB(9,17)"4 VIEW GRAPH"
1190 PRINTTAB(9,22)"CHOOSE A NUMBER"
1200 REPEAT
1210    Z=GET
1220    UNTIL Z>48 AND Z<53
1230 IF Z=49 THEN PROC_restart:
     PROC_input
1240 IF Z=50 AND N>1 THEN PROC_forecast
1250 IF Z=51 AND flag=1 THEN
     PROC_display
1260 IF Z=52 AND flag=1 AND N>1
     THEN PROC_graph
1270 ENDPROC
1280
1290 DEFPROC_init
1300 VDU19,0,4;0;
1310 VDU23,224,0,&7E,&7E,&7E,&7E,&7E,
     &7E,0
1320 VDU23,225,&FF,&81,&81,&81,&81,&81,
     &81,&FF
1330 DIMmonth(36),fcast(36)
1340 N=0:flag=0
1350 ENDPROC
1360
1370 DEFPROC_restart
1380 topval=-99999:botval=99999
1390 maxval=99999:minval=-99999
1400 sm=0:nsq=0:sv=0:vsq=0:so=0
1410 N=0
1420 flag=0
1430 ENDPROC
1440
1450 DEFPROC_input
```

```
1460 CLS
1470 PRINTTAB(15,1)"DATA ENTRY"
1480 PRINTTAB(0,3)STRING$(40,"*")
1490 PRINTTAB(4,5)
     "ENTER VALUES FOR EACH MONTH"
1500 PRINTTAB(4,6)
     "PRESS [RETURN] WHEN FINISHED"
1510 PRINT
1520 N=0
1530 REPEAT
1540   N=N+1
1550   PRINTN;
1560   INPUT") "month$
1570   month(N)=VAL(month$):fcast(N)=0
1580   UNTILmonth$=""
1590 N=N-1
1600 PROC_coef
1610 ENDPROC
1620
1630 DEFPROC_coef
1640 flag=1
1650 FORP=1TON
1660   monthval=month(P)
1670   IF monthval<maxval THEN
       maxval=monthval
1680   IF monthval>minval THEN
       minval=monthval
1690   sm=sm+P:sv=sv+monthval
1700   so=so+P*monthval
1710   nsq=nsq+P^2
1720   vsq=vsq+monthval^2
1730   NEXT P
1740 IF N*nsq-sm*sm<=0 THEN coef=0:
     startval=0
1750 IF N*nsq-sm*sm<=0 THEN explvar=0
1760 IF N*nsq-sm*sm<=0 THEN percentvar=
     0:ENDPROC
1770 startval=(nsq*sv-sm*so)/
     (N*nsq-sm*sm)
1780 coef=(N*so-sm*sv)/(N*nsq-sm*sm)
1790 IF (N*nsq-sm*sm)*(N*vsq-sv*sv)=0
     THEN explvar=1
1800 IF (N*nsq-sm*sm)*(N*vsq-sv*sv)=0
     THEN percentvar=100:ENDPROC
```

```
1810 explvar=(N*so-sm*sv)/
     SQR((N*nsq-sm*sm)*(N*vsq-sv*sv))
1820 percentvar=100*explvar*explvar
1830 ENDPROC
1840
1850 DEFPROC_forecast
1860 CLS
1870 @%=&20209
1880 PRINTTAB(15,1)"FORECAST"
1890 PRINTTAB(0,3)STRING$(40,"*")
1900 PRINTTAB(2,6)
     "CHANGE PER MONTH         = "coef
1910 PRINTTAB(2,8)
     "STARTING VALUE           = "
     startval
1920 PRINTTAB(2,10)
     "VARIANCE EXPLAINED       = "
     percentvar"%"
1930 PRINTTAB(2,12)
     "HIGHEST VALUE OF DATA    = "maxval
1940 PRINTTAB(2,14)
     "LOWEST  VALUE OF DATA    = "minval
1950 @%=&10
1960 PRINTTAB(4,20)
     "PRESS SPACE BAR TO CONTINUE"
1970 REPEAT
1980    Z$=GET$
1990    UNTIL Z$=" "
2000 ENDPROC
2010
2020 DEFPROC_display
2030 CLS
2040 @%=&20209
2050 PRINTTAB(12,1)"PROJECTED VALUES"
2060 PRINTTAB(0,3)STRING$(40,"*")
2070 PRINTTAB(2,5)
     "MONTH       ACTUAL       FORECAST"
2080 FOR X=1TO18
2090    PRINTTAB(4,X+5)STR$X
2100    IFX<=N THEN PRINTTAB(18,X+5)
     STR$(month(X))
2110    PRINTTAB(25,X+5)coef*X+startval
2120    NEXT X
2130 PRINT"PRESS SPACE BAR TO CONTINUE"
```

```
2140 REPEAT
2150    Z$=GET$
2160    UNTIL Z$=" "
2170 CLS
2180 PRINTTAB(12,1)"PROJECTED VALUES"
2190 PRINTTAB(0,3)STRING$(40,"*")
2200 PRINTTAB(2,5)
     "MONTH        ACTUAL        FORECAST"
2210 FOR X=19TO36
2220    PRINTTAB(4,X-13)STR$X
2230    IFX<=N THEN PRINTTAB(18,X-13)
     STR$(month(X))
2240    PRINTTAB(25,X-13)coef*X+startval
2250    NEXT X
2260 @%=&10
2270 PRINT"PRESS SPACE BAR TO CONTINUE"
2280 REPEAT
2290    Z$=GET$
2300    UNTIL Z$=" "
2310 ENDPROC
2320
2330 DEFPROC_graph
2340 REPEAT
2350    CLS
2360    PRINTTAB(6,8)
        "ENTER A TITLE FOR THE GRAPH"
2370    INPUTtitle$
2380    UNTIL LEN(title$)<40
2390 CLS
2400 MOVE92,1023
2410 DRAW92,100
2420 MOVE0,100
2430 DRAW1280,100
2440 start=(40-LEN(title$))/2
2450 PRINTTAB(15,1)"PROJECTION"
2460 PRINTTAB(start,3)title$
2470 PRINTTAB(0,29)"MONTHS->"
2480 PRINTTAB(3,30)"1"TAB(13,30)"12"
     TAB(25,30)"24"TAB(37,30)"36";
2490 COLOUR2
2500 PRINTTAB(1,31)
     "ACTUAL VALUES-> "CHR$224;
2510 PRINTTAB(19,31)
     "PROJECTED VALUES->"CHR$225;
```

```
2520 COLOUR3
2530 FORX=1TO36
2540   fcast(X)=coef*X+startval
2550   IFfcast(X)>topval THEN topval=
       fcast(X)
2560   IFfcast(X)<botval THEN botval=
       fcast(X)
2570   NEXT
2580 IF minval>topval THENtopval=minval
2590 IF maxval<botval THENbotval=maxval
2600 IF botval>0 THEN scale=10/topval
     ELSE scale=20/(topval-botval)
2610 IF botval<0 AND topval<0 THEN
     scale=20/ABS(botval)
2620 COLOUR2
2630 gr$=CHR$224
2640 FORX=1TON
2650   grval=month(X)*scale+
       ABS(botval*scale)
2660   IF INT(month(X)*scale)>-1 THEN
       PROC_plus ELSE PROC_minus
2670   COLOUR3
2680   NEXT X
2690 FORX=N+1TO36
2700   grval=fcast(X)*scale+
       ABS(botval*scale)
2710   IF INT(fcast(X)*scale)>-1 THEN
       PROC_plus ELSE PROC_minus
2720   COLOUR3
2730   NEXT X
2740 MOVE0,(INT(ABS(botval*scale))+5)*
     32
2750 DRAW1279,
     (INT(ABS(botval*scale))+5)*32
2760 ptab=
         27-INT(ABS(botval*scale))
2770 PRINTTAB(1,ptab)"0"
2780 Z$=GET$
2790 ENDPROC
2800
2810 DEFPROC_plus
2820 IF X>N THEN gr$=CHR$225
2830 COLOUR2
2840   FORY=(ABS(botval*scale))TOgrval
```

```
2850    PRINTTAB(X+2,27-Y)gr$
2860    NEXT Y
2870 ENDPROC
2880
2890 DEFPROC_minus
2900 IF X>N THEN gr$=CHR$225
2910 COLOUR1
2920 FOR Y%=grval TO
        INT(ABS(botval*scale))
2930    PRINTTAB(X+2,27-Y%)gr$
2940    NEXT Y%
2950 ENDPROC
```

Notes on the program

Lines 1040–1090 contain the first module. **Lines 1040** and **1050** set the mode to 1, and change the colour of the text to green.

PROC_menu provides the choice screen with four options: entering data, producing a forecast, displaying forecast of future months and viewing a graph.

Lines 1200–1220 contain a routine that checks to ensure that the key pressed lies between the accepted values. The variable 'flag' checks that information has been entered before calculations are performed.

PROC_init sets the background to blue, defines a solid block 7×7 pixels in size and a hollow block in **lines 1310** and **1320**, and reserves space for the actual and predicted values.

PROC_restart sets the initial values of variables used in the calculations each time fresh data is entered.

PROC_input allows the input of data by using a REPEAT loop. This repeats until an empty string is entered by the user pressing only the RETURN key. The actual values are stored in array month(N), while each predicted value is reset to 0 in array fcast(N). The loop counter N records how many months have been entered.

PROC_coef calculates the explained variance in a similar manner to that used in the previous program by using the sums of squares method for the values obtained each month.

Line 1770 calculates the imagined starting value or origin of the graph, assuming that the line is straight, and puts the value in variable 'startval'.

Line 1780 calculates by how much the values increase or decrease each month and puts the value in variable 'coef'. This value determines the slope of the graph.

Line 1820 calculates the variance expressed as a percentage and puts the value in variable 'percentvar'.

PROC_forecast simply prints out the explained variance as well as the maximum and minimum values of data. If the explained variance is less than 50 or 60 per cent, the prediction is unlikely to be very accurate (as explained in the text before this program).

Line 1870 restricts the number display to two decimal places, and **line 1950** resets the formatting to the original value. This method is also used in **lines 2040** and **2260** in PROC_display.

PROC_display prints the actual values that have been entered as well as the predicted values for a three-year period. This is done in two blocks of 18 months, so that the display fits on the screen without scrolling. The actual values are given by month(X) at this stage, and the predicted values from the formula:

predicted value = coef*X+startval

The predicted values are not loaded into the array fcast(X) until PROC_graph.

PROC_graph allows a title to be entered and the graph is displayed showing solid blocks for actual values, and hollow blocks for predicted values.

Line 2440 formats the title so that it is positioned in the middle of the line no matter how many characters it contains. **Line 2480** provides an indication of the numbers of the months.

Lines 2530–2570 contain the loop where the predicted values are loaded into the array fcast(X).

Lines 2640–2680 draw the graph on actual values.

Lines 2690–2730 draw the graph using the predicted values.

Lines 2740–2770 determine where the zero line will be drawn and position it on the screen.

PROC_plus draws the blocks on the graph if the values are positive.

PROC_minus draws the blocks if the values are negative gr$ is a solid block for actual values and a hollow block for predicted values.

CHAPTER 6
Home Education

Education and learning

The Electron is an ideal computer to help with education in the home. One of the main reasons for this is the fact that it uses the same version of BASIC as the BBC micro, the most popular computer in both primary and secondary schools in the UK. Children who use a BBC micro at school can continue to improve their skills at home, and are less likely to pick up poor programming habits by using an inferior copy of BASIC.

Many programs that are termed educational simply use the computer as a sort of electronic blackboard and do not exploit the features that make the computer unique. A typical program might print a long multiplication sum on the screen and accept input for the different stages involved. If the child enters the correct response, the sum is marked right; but if a response is incorrect, the program either loops round until by chance the correct number is chosen, or else the sum is marked wrong and the next one appears. This sort of program is only useful to test present knowledge, and little actual learning takes place. It would be far easier to sit the child down with pencil and paper.

What is the alternative to this sort of program? If your definition of educational is fairly wide, almost anything else! Many adventure programs are far more educational in that they let the user set up a hypothesis and test it out, eg 'What will happen if I attempt to kill the dragon with a sword?' If 'educational' is taken to mean that which encourages the user to learn more, then it is easier to avoid the type of programs that feel more like 'go to your room and don't come down until you can recite all your tables backwards!'

In this chapter I shall look at some ways in which Acorn machines can help with learning in the home. The first is a multi-purpose quiz program that could help with any subject in which facts are important, or it could be adapted to help with spellings or even maths problems. Next, I shall look at an unusual way to approach the multiplication example I gave earlier, and then there is a rather more practical program to speed up your keyboard skills. If you are interested in programs in particular areas of education, Sunshine Books publish a series by Patrick Hall and myself called Programming for Education (mentioned earlier in this book).

The first program in this chapter is a general quiz program that can be

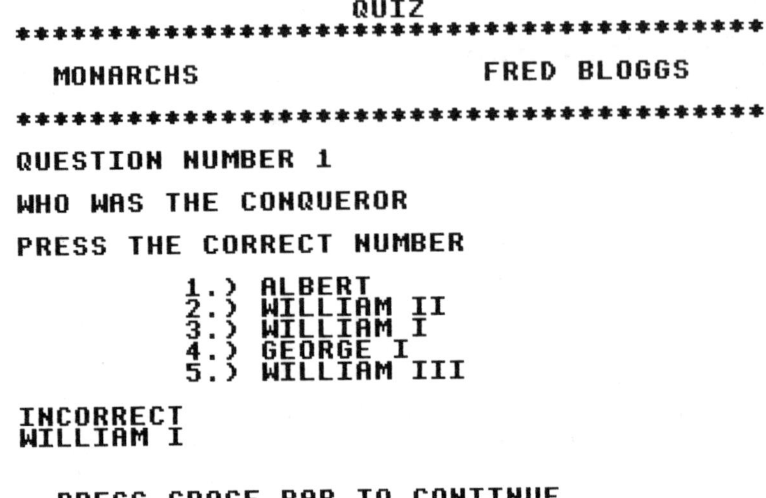

Figure 6.1: Screen Dump from Quiz.

used in general knowledge competitions, as a test, or as a revision aid before exams. The program itself provides a standard framework, and the questions and answers are loaded separately from a file held on cassette or disk. In this way, the same program can be used with a variety of subjects, and the length and difficulty can be graded with ease. The initial menu allows you to choose from several options: to design a new quiz, to save it on file, to answer a quiz already in memory, or to load a fresh one from tape. Users enter their names and the final score is shown on screen.

The format chosen is multi-choice, sometimes referred to as the alternative answer approach. The five possible answers can be chosen to make the choice difficult or easy, and the answers only require one key to be pressed, making it suitable in cases where speed is important, or where the user finds writing difficult.

Quiz

```
1000 REM   ***      QUIZ        ***
1010 REM
1020 REM   *** AJS 10/2/83   ***
1030
1040 MODE6
```

```
1050 PROC_init
1060
1070 REPEAT
1080    PROC_menu
1090    UNTIL FALSE
1100
1110 DEFPROC_init
1120 VDU19,0,4;0;
1130 flag=0
1140 mix$="12345"
1150 ENDPROC
1160
1170 DEFPROC_menu
1180 CLS
1190 PRINTTAB(17,1)"QUIZ"
1200 PRINTTAB(0,3)STRING$(40,"*")
1210 PRINTTAB(4,5)"1 DESIGN A QUIZ"
1220 PRINTTAB(4,7)"2 RUN THE QUIZ"
1230 PRINTTAB(4,9)"3 LOAD A QUIZ"
1240 PRINTTAB(4,11)"4 SAVE A QUIZ"
1250 PRINTTAB(4,13)"5 STOP THE PROGRAM"
1260 PRINTTAB(4,16)"CHOOSE A NUMBER"
1270 REPEAT
1280    Z$=GET$
1290    Z=VAL(Z$)
1300    UNTIL Z>0 AND Z<6
1310 IF Z=1 THEN PROC_makequiz
1320 IF Z=2 AND flag=1 THENPROC_runquiz
1330 IF Z=3 THEN PROC_load
1340 IF Z=4 AND flag=1 THEN PROC_save
1350 IF Z=5 THEN STOP
1360 ENDPROC
1370
1380 DEFPROC_makequiz
1390 CLS
1400 *FX21,0
1410 Z$=""
1420 IF flag=1 THEN PRINTTAB(7,2)
     "QUIZ FILE ALREADY PRESENT"
1430 IF flag=1 THEN PRINTTAB(6,4)
     "PRESS SPACE BAR TO CONTINUE"
1440 IF flag=1 THEN Z$=GET$
1450 IF flag=1 THEN ENDPROC
1460 PRINTTAB(12,1)"DESIGN A QUIZ"
```

```
1470 PRINTTAB(0,2)STRING$(40,"*")
1480 PRINTTAB(0,5)
     "ENTER A NAME FOR THE QUIZ"
1490 INPUT name$
1500 PRINTTAB(0,7)
     "HOW MANY QUESTIONS ARE THERE?"
1510 REPEAT
1520    INPUT number
1530    UNTIL number>0
1540 DIM question$(number)
1550 DIM answer$(number,5)
1560 DIM correctnum(number)
1570 PRINTTAB(0,11)
     "YOU CAN NOW ENTER THE QUESTIONS"
1580 PRINTTAB(0,13)
     "AND THE ALTERNATIVE ANSWERS"
1590 PRINTTAB(0,15)
     "PRESS SPACE BAR WHEN READY"
1600 Z$=GET$
1610 FOR N = 1 TO number
1620    REPEAT
1630       CLS
1640       PRINTTAB(0,1)
           "QUESTION NUMBER ";N
1650       PRINTTAB(0,2)STRING$(40,"*")
1660       PRINTTAB(0,4)
           "ENTER THE QUESTION"
1670       INPUTTAB(0,5)question$(N)
1680       PRINTTAB(0,8)
           "ENTER ALTERNATIVE ANSWERS"
1690       FOR X=1TO5
1700          PRINTX;
1710          INPUT,answer$(N,X)
1720          NEXT X
1730       PRINT
           "ENTER NO. OF CORRECT ANSWER"
1740       INPUT correctnum(N)
1750       PRINT"IS THIS CORRECT?"
1760       Z$=GET$
1770       UNTIL Z$="Y"
1780    NEXT N
1790 flag=1
1800 ENDPROC
1810
```

```
1820 DEFPROC_runquiz
1830 score = 0
1840 CLS
1850 PRINTTAB(18,1)"QUIZ"
1860 PRINTTAB(0,2)STRING$(40,"*")
1870 len=LEN(name$)
1880 PRINTTAB(2,4)name$
1890 PRINTTAB(0,6)STRING$(40,"*")
1900 PRINT"ENTER YOUR NAME"
1910 INPUT username$
1920 PRINTTAB(25,4)username$
1930 VDU28,0,24,39,8
1940 CLS
1950 FOR N=1 TO number
1960    PROC_mix
1970    PRINT"QUESTION NUMBER ";N
1980    PRINT
1990    PRINTquestion$(N)
2000    PRINT
2010    PRINT"PRESS THE CORRECT NUMBER"
2020    PRINT
2030    FOR X=1 TO 5
2040       PRINTX;".) ";
          answer$(N,VAL(MID$(mix$,X,1)))
2050       NEXT X
2060    PRINT
2070    REPEAT
2080       Z$ = GET$
2090       guess = VAL(Z$)
2100       UNTIL guess>0 AND guess <6
2110    IF guess=pos THEN score=score+1
2120    IF guess=pos THEN PRINT
       "CORRECT" ELSE PRINT"INCORRECT"
2130    IF guess <> pos THEN PRINT
       answer$(N,correctnum(N))
2140    PRINTTAB(2,16)
       "PRESS SPACE BAR TO CONTINUE";
2150    Z$=GET$
2160    CLS
2170    NEXT N
2180 CLS
2190 PRINTusername$;" SCORED ";score;
     " OUT OF ";number
2200 PRINT
```

```
2210 PRINT"PRESS SPACE BAR TO CONTINUE"
2220 Z$=GET$
2230 VDU26
2240 ENDPROC
2250
2260 DEFPROC_save
2270 CLS
2280 PRINTTAB(12,1)"SAVING A QUIZ"
2290 PRINTTAB(0,2)STRING$(40,"*")
2300 PRINTTAB(0,4)"ENTER THE FILE NAME"
2310 INPUT file$
2320 PRINTTAB(0,8)"SAVING "file$
2330 x%=OPENOUT(file$)
2340 PRINT#x%,name$
2350 PRINT#x%,number
2360 FOR N = 1 TO number
2370    PRINT#x%,question$(N)
2380    FOR X=1TO5
2390      PRINT#x%,answer$(N,X)
2400      PRINT#x%,correctnum(N)
2410      NEXT X
2420    NEXT N
2430 CLOSE#x%
2440 ENDPROC
2450
2460 DEFPROC_load
2470 CLS
2480 PRINTTAB(12,1)"LOADING A QUIZ"
2490 PRINTTAB(0,2)STRING$(40,"*")
2500 PRINTTAB(0,4)"ENTER THE FILE NAME"
2510 INPUT file$
2520 PRINTTAB(0,8)"LOADING "file$
2530 x%=OPENIN(file$)
2540 INPUT#x%,name$
2550 INPUT#x%,number
2560 DIM question$(number)
2570 DIM answer$(number,5)
2580 DIM correctnum(number)
2590 FOR N = 1 TO number
2600    INPUT#x%,question$(N)
2610    FOR X=1TO5
2620      INPUT#x%,answer$(N,X)
2630      INPUT#x%,correctnum(N)
2640      NEXT X
```

```
2650    NEXT N
2660 CLOSE#x%
2670 flag=1
2680 ENDPROC
2690
2700 DEFPROC_mix
2710 mix$=""
2720 X$="12345"
2730 FOR X=1 TO 5
2740    IF RND(2)=1 THEN mix$=mix$+
        MID$(X$,X,1) ELSE mix$=
        MID$(X$,X,1)+mix$
2750    NEXT X
2760 cnum$=STR$(correctnum(N))
2770 pos=INSTR(mix$,cnum$)
2780 ENDPROC
```

Notes on the program

Line 1040 sets the mode for the program. You are not allowed to change mode inside a procedure, which is why it is done here.

PROC_init sets the variables to their starting values. The VDU statement sets the background colour to blue. I find this fairly restful, but you can replace the 4 by another colour number if you wish.

PROC_menu is a standard menu of choices. The keyboard is scanned in **lines 1270–1300** until a key with a value between 1 and 5 is pressed. The variable 'flag' is used to make sure you can't run or save a non-existent quiz file.

PROC_makequiz clears the screen and uses *FX 21,0 to clear all input buffers. Variable 'flag' is used again to test if a file is already present. If you want to design a quiz you will have to choose option 5 — stop the program — and run it again.

The subsequent lines in the program allow you to enter the home name and the number of questions, so that memory can be reserved for the questions and answers. **Lines 1540–1560** reserve this space.

Note that if you load a different quiz file from tape after designing one, you will get an error message when the computer attempts to redimension space for the arrays in PROC_load. Use option 5 from the main menu to avoid this happening.

Lines 1610–1780 contain a large loop to allow the input of the questions and the five alternative answers. As you can see, it's not difficult to alter the number of alternatives in **lines 1550**, **1690** and **2570** although five choices is about the right number for most applications.

Line 1790 sets 'flag' equal to 1 to show that a quiz file is now resident.

At this stage you are sent back to the main menu, and you can try out the quiz before committing it to tape or disk.

PROC_runquiz prints the names of the quiz, name$, and the user, username$, at the top of the screen, then defines a text window in **line 1930**. All printing will now take place inside this window, and the main information remains intact at the top of the screen.

Lines 1950–2170 contain the question loop and also check the accuracy of each response.

In **line 2040**, the alternative answers are printed in the order of the rearranged string, so instead of the answers always being shown in the same order, there is some variety. In **line 2130**, the input 'guess' is compared with the correct answer, 'pos'.

Line 2190 prints the score achieved by the user. It would be easy to store the name of the user and their score in a previously-dimensioned array at this point, so that a parent or teacher could check on the scores at a later stage. You could also store the guesses, so that particular weaknesses could be traced.

Line 2230 resets the text window back to normal, ie the whole screen is used for text.

PROC_mix is contained in **lines 2700–2780**. This procedure rearranges the X$ ('12345') in **line 2740** to form mix$. This could end up as something like '25314'.

Lines 2760 and **2770** find the position of the correct answer inside this string, eg if 1 was the correct answer, it would have been at position 4 in the above example, and this value is loaded into variable 'pos'.

PROC_save lets you save a written quiz. You choose a file name and it opens a channel to the cassette or disk and stores the quiz name, number of questions, actual questions, alternative answers and correct response.

PROC_load loads in a previously-saved quiz file. Each line in this procedure has an equivalent in PROC_save except **line 2670** which sets variable 'flag' to 1 to show that a quiz file is resident in the memory.

Remember the warning about stopping the program before loading in a new quiz file to avoid error messages.

Long multiplication

The next program is based on the sure knowledge that some things we need to learn can be terribly boring, and anything to relieve this boredom not only makes the subject more interesting — it also encourages a better atmosphere for learning.

The subject in question is long multiplication, and the program demonstrates a rather interesting way of coping with large numbers if you can't remember your tables and can't find the calculator. It is attributed to poor peasants in pre-revolutionary Russia who could just about cope with halving and doubling, and so is often known as Russian multiplication, although it is imagined that Soyuz cosmonauts use something rather more elaborate to calculate their orbits!

The system works like this: take the two numbers you want to multiply, eg 21 and 43, and write them down. Now halve the first number and double the second, and write the answers under the original numbers, ignoring any halves. Repeat this process until you have a one in the first column. This is what you should get:

```
21        43
10        86
 5       172
 2       344
 1       688
```

Next, you look down the numbers in the first column and note those that are odd. Now you add together the numbers in the *second* column that are opposite the odd numbers in the first column. This gives you this result:

```
21        43*
10        86
 5       172*
 2       344
 1       688*
```

Adding together the marked numbers:

```
          43
         172
         688
         ___
         903
```

If you check, 21 × 43 really is 903. This method is the sort of thing that surprises people, and is something to relieve boring evenings in the pub when you scribble it out on the back of an envelope. (It will either amaze your friends, or the barman will throw you out for passing betting slips!)

You may like to consider why this method works, and why it is an ideal subject for computers. If you try it out with numbers like 128 (2 to the power of 7) or 127 (one less than 2 to the power of 7), you should be able to see why.

Boris

```
1000 REM **            BORIS            **
1010 REM
1020 REM **     A.J.S.  5/8/83       **
1030
1040 MODE1
1050 COLOUR130:COLOUR1
1060 REPEAT
1070    CLS
1080    PRINTTAB(16,1)"RUSSIAN"
1090    PRINTTAB(12,2)"MULTIPLICATION"
1100    PRINTTAB(0,3)STRING$(40,"*");
1110    PRINT"ENTER TWO NUMBERS"
1120    PRINT
1130    INPUT"FIRST  NUMBER - "A
1140    INPUT"SECOND NUMBER - "B
1150    PRINT
1160    PRINT"THE SUM IS ";A;" X ";B
1170    PRINTTAB(0,11)STRING$(40,"*")
1180    SUM=0
1190    REPEAT
1200       PRINTA,B;
1210       IF A MOD 2 = 1 THEN SUM=SUM+B
1220       IF A MOD 2 = 1 THEN PRINT
              "*"ELSE PRINT
1230       PRINT
1240       A=INT(A/2)
1250       B=B*2
1260       UNTIL A<2
1270    PRINTA,B;
1280    IF A MOD 2 = 1 THEN SUM=SUM+B
1290    IF A MOD 2 = 1 THEN PRINT"*"
1300    PRINT
1310    PRINT"ADD ALL NOS. MARKED '*'"
1320    PRINT
```

```
1330    PRINT"ANSWER  = "SUM
1340    PRINT
1350    PRINTTAB(2,31)
        "PRESS SPACE BAR TO REPEAT";
1360    Z$=GET$
1370    UNTIL FALSE
```

Notes on the program

Lines 1060–1370 contain the main loop. As the program is very short, there are no procedures.

Lines 1130 and **1140** allow the input of two numbers. There is no input check here — if the second number contains a fraction, the method can cope, as it will be doubled up with no problems. If the first number contains a fraction however, when it is halved, any remainder is ignored, so the final result will be inaccurate.

Lines 1280 and **1290** use the MOD function to check if the first number is even or odd. If A MOD2 = 1, then A is odd; if A MOD2 = 0, then A is even.

Variable 'sum' contains the total and prints the answer at **line 1330**.

Keyboard skills

The next program in this chapter is designed to help you improve your keyboard skills. Although voice recognition chips and computer mice may one day make keyboard entry a thing of the past, it is unlikely to occur for some years. Learning to touch-type is something that can be speeded up by using a computer, and the results should be worth all the trouble of typing the program in.

When you learn to type, you are first introduced to the home keys, the bases from which you explore the rest of the keyboard. It is therefore useful to learn the position of the keys in the early stages, and to know which ones you are touching. The first part of the program is concerned with simple letter location, and is written in mode 2. A large copy of the keyboard appears in the top half of the screen, and when a key is touched, it lights up on the display. Letters and numbers are selected at random, and printed in the centre of the screen, and your performance is timed. At present you are only given five letters — this should obviously be increased to about 50, so you can check if your speed increases.

It is a good idea to avoid looking at the keyboard while using this program. In fact, you probably won't improve unless you do this, but it's easier said than done, and typing schools often have keys with the letters, etc, removed. If you consider this a little drastic, one idea is to cut a side out of a shoe box. This can be placed over the keyboard and your hands will fit under it. It is a pity that Acorn computers don't have dimples on a couple of the home keys, as some computers do, as this would make touch-typing much easier.

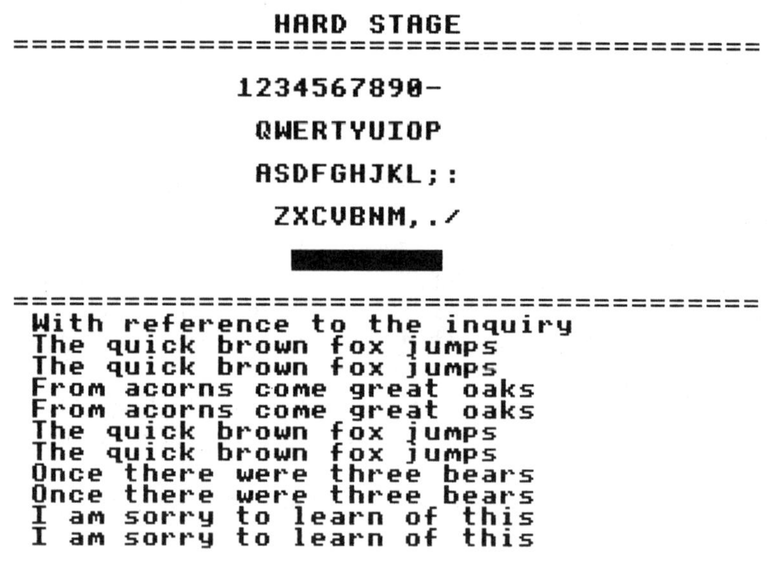

Figure 6.2: Screen Dump from Typist.

Once you know where the keys are, you can go on to the next section — easy words. These are arranged in order of difficulty, and are selected according to the difficulty level you choose at the start. The screen is split into two sections, as in the first section, but this time mode 1 is used. A small copy of the keyboard appears at the top to remind you of the key positions. Words are chosen at random and appear in the lower half in green. If the key you touch is correct, the letter will appear in red underneath the original. If it is incorrect, the word MISTAKE will appear, and the next word will appear.

The first 20 words in the data statements are made up from letters in the centre row of the keyboard, and later words use letters further away from the home keys. It is a simple matter to alter the data lines to include whatever words you like, and there is plenty of room in the memory to store a hundred or so more words.

The final section of the program gives you whole sentences to copy, and uses a similar routine to the last section. Again, you are timed, and mistakes are shown clearly on the screen.

One point that should be made is that it is important to have CAPS LOCK *on* during the first section, as key position is the learning theme, but *off* in sections 2 and 3, as you will need both upper and lower case.

Typist

```
1000 REM **     TYPIST     **
1010 REM
1020 REM **   AJS 2/2/84   **
1030
1040 MODE1
1050 PROC_init
1060 PROC_instr
1070 REPEAT
1080    MODE1
1090    PROC_menu
1100    IFZ=49THEN MODE2:PROC_learn
1110    IFZ=50THEN MODE1:PROC_easy
1120    IFZ=51THEN MODE1:PROC_hard
1130    UNTIL FALSE
1140
1150 DEFPROC_init
1160 VDU23,224,&FF,&FF,&FF,&FF,&FF,&FF,
     &FF,&FF
1170 one$="1234567890-"
1180 two$="QWERTYUIOP"
1190 three$="ASDFGHJKL;:"
1200 four$="ZXCVBNM,./"
1210 space$=STRING$(8,CHR$224)
1220 VDU19,0,4;0;
1230 ENDPROC
1240
1250 DEFPROC_instr
1260 PRINTTAB(12,5)"TYPING TUTOR"
1270 PRINTTAB(0,7)STRING$(40,"*")
1280 PRINTTAB(5)
     "CHOOSE LETTER RECOGNITION"
1290 PRINT
1300 PRINTTAB(7)"OR WORDS OR SENTENCES"
1310 PRINT
1320 PRINTTAB(4)
     "REMEMBER TO HAVE CAPS LOCK"
1330 PRINT
1340 PRINTTAB(10)"ON FOR LETTERS"
1350 PRINT
1360 PRINTTAB(7)"AND OFF FOR WORDS AND"
1370 PRINT
1380 PRINTTAB(12)"SENTENCES"
```

```
1390  PRINT
1400  PRINTTAB(9)"PRESS SPACE BAR"
1410  Z$ = GET$
1420  ENDPROC
1430
1440  DEFPROC_menu
1450  CLS
1460  PRINTTAB(18,3)"MENU"
1470  PRINTTAB(5,6)"1 LEARN KEYS"
1480  PRINTTAB(5,8)"2 EASY TUTOR"
1490  PRINTTAB(5,10)"3 HARD TUTOR"
1500  PRINTTAB(5,14)
      "PRESS THE NUMBER OF YOUR CHOICE"
1510  REPEAT
1520     Z=GET
1530     UNTILZ>48ANDZ<52
1540  ENDPROC
1550
1560  DEFPROC_key
1570  VDU26
1580  PRINTTAB(3,4)one$
1590  PRINTTAB(4,6)two$
1600  PRINTTAB(4,8)three$
1610  PRINTTAB(5,10)four$
1620  PRINTTAB(6,12)space$
1630  PRINTTAB(1,15)"PRESS THE LETTER -"
1640  ENDPROC
1650
1660  DEFPROC_learn
1670  VDU19,7,2;0;
1680  starttime=TIME
1690  PROC_key
1700  FOR N = 1 TO 5
1710     REPEAT
1720        VDU28,0,31,19,18
1730        letter=RND(43)+47
1740        UNTIL letter<60 OR letter>64
1750     letter$=CHR$(letter)
1760     PRINTTAB(9,0)letter$
1770     REPEAT
1780        Z$=GET$
1790        PROC_key
1800        PROC_show
1810        VDU28,0,31,17,18
```

```
1820        UNTILZ$=letter$
1830    NEXT N
1840 timetaken=TIME-starttime
1850 timesecs=timetaken DIV 100
1860 PRINTTAB(0,2)"TIME TAKEN = "
1870 PRINTTAB(0,4)timesecs" SECONDS"
1880 PRINTTAB(0,6)"PRESS SPACE BAR"
1890 Z$ = GET$
1900 ENDPROC
1910
1920 DEFPROC_show
1930 VDU26
1940 COLOUR9
1950 Z=0:flag=0
1960 pos=INSTR(one$,Z$)
1970 IF pos<>0 THEN PROC_print(pos+2,4)
1980 pos=INSTR(two$,Z$)
1990 IF pos<>0 THEN PROC_print(pos+3,6)
2000 pos=INSTR(three$,Z$)
2010 IF pos<>0 THEN PROC_print(pos+3,8)
2020 pos=INSTR(four$,Z$)
2030 IF pos<>0THEN PROC_print(pos+4,10)
2040 COLOUR7
2050 ENDPROC
2060
2070 DEFPROC_print(x,y)
2080 PRINTTAB(x,y)Z$
2090 ENDPROC
2100
2110 DEFPROC_easy
2115 score = 0
2120 VDU19,7,2;0;
2130 PRINTTAB(14,1)"EASY STAGE"
2140 PRINTTAB(0,2)STRING$(40,"=");
2150 PRINTTAB(12,4)one$
2160 PRINTTAB(13,6)two$
2170 PRINTTAB(13,8)three$
2180 PRINTTAB(14,10)four$
2190 PRINTTAB(15,12)space$
2200 PRINTTAB(0,14)STRING$(40,"=");
2210 PRINT"ENTER DIFFICULTY, 1-5"
2220 REPEAT
2230    diff$ = GET$
2240    diff = VAL(diff$)
```

```
2250    UNTIL diff>0 AND diff<6
2260 PRINTTAB(30,4)"DIFFICULTY"
2270 PRINTTAB(25,5)diff
2280 VDU28,0,30,39,15
2290 starttime=TIME
2300 PRINTTAB(2,2)
2310 FOR go = 1 TO 10
2320   RESTORE 3010
2330   FOR N = 1 TO RND(diff*10)
2340     READ word$
2350     NEXT N
2360   PRINTTAB(15) word$
2370   count = 0
2380   PRINTTAB(15);
2390   REPEAT
2400     count=count+1
2410     Z$ = GET$
2420     COLOUR 1
2430     PRINTZ$;
2440     COLOUR 7
2450     UNTIL Z$<>MID$(word$,count,1)
         OR count = LEN(word$)
2460   IF Z$<>MID$(word$,count,1) THEN
       PRINT"MISTAKE"ELSEscore=score+1
2470   PRINT
2480   NEXT go
2490 PRINT
2500 PRINT"SCORE = "score
2510 timetaken=TIME-starttime
2520 timesecs=timetaken DIV 100
2530 PRINT"TIME TAKEN = "timesecs
     " SECONDS"
2540 PRINT"PRESS SPACE BAR"
2550 Z$ = GET$
2560 ENDPROC
2570
2580 DEFPROC_hard
2585 score = 0
2590 VDU19,7,2;0;
2600 PRINTTAB(14,1)"HARD STAGE"
2610 PRINTTAB(0,2)STRING$(40,"=");
2620 PRINTTAB(12,4)one$
2630 PRINTTAB(13,6)two$
2640 PRINTTAB(13,8)three$
```

```
2650 PRINTTAB(14,10)four$
2660 PRINTTAB(15,12)space$
2670 PRINTTAB(0,14)STRING$(40,"=");
2680 starttime=TIME
2690 VDU28,0,30,39,15
2700 FOR go = 1 TO 10
2710   RESTORE 3150
2720   FOR N = 1 TO RND(10)
2730     READ sentence$
2740     NEXT N
2750   PRINTTAB(1) sentence$
2760   count = 0
2770   PRINTTAB(1);
2780   REPEAT
2790     count=count+1
2800     Z$ = GET$
2810     COLOUR 1
2820     PRINTZ$;
2830     COLOUR 7
2840     UNTIL Z$ <>
         MID$(sentence$,count,1)
         OR count = LEN(sentence$)
2850   IF Z$ <> MID$(sentence$,count,1)
       THEN PRINT"MISTAKE" ELSE
       score=score+1
2860   PRINT
2870   NEXT go
2880 PRINT
2890 PRINT"SCORE = "score
2900 timetaken=TIME-starttime
2910 timesecs=timetaken DIV 100
2920 PRINT"TIME TAKEN = "timesecs
     " SECONDS"
2930 PRINT"PRESS SPACE BAR"
2940 Z$ = GET$
2950 ENDPROC
2960
2970 REM ** WORDS ARRANGED IN ORDER **
2980 REM **       OF DIFFICULTY       **
2990 REM **  (THERE ARE FIFTY HERE)  **
3000
3010 DATA sad,had,fad,lad,sag,lag,fag
3020 DATA kag,jag,hag,fal,gal,dal,sal
3030 DATA flag,glad,fags,lads,gaff,lash
```

```
3040 DATA the,you,how,three,four,truth
3050 DATA grit,hut,jut,rut,our,try,let
3060 DATA cry,buy,bat,gin,hen,mud,sin
3070 DATA carry,dart,enough,begin
3080 DATA engine,lorry,road,street
3090 DATA follow,stop,work,ending
3100 DATA just,cart,this,that
3110 DATA think,fight,borrow,start
3120
3130 REM **      SENTENCES      **
3140
3150 DATA The quick brown fox jumps
3160 DATA Dear sir or madam
3170 DATA With reference to the inquiry
3180 DATA From acorns come great oaks
3190 DATA Friday is better than Monday
3200 DATA I am sorry to learn of this
3210 DATA Please read the enclosed note
3220 DATA 1 High St Newcastle Upon Tyne
3230 DATA This is written in ITV BASIC
3240 DATA Once there were three bears
```

Notes on the program

Lines 1040–1130 contain the control module. The way this is set out is due to the inability to change modes inside a procedure.

PROC_init contains definitions to help with the display of the keyboard on the screen. **Line 1160** defines a solid block using VDU 23. The strings in **lines 1170–1210** are to save entering the key letters each time. **Line 1220** sets the background colour to blue.

PROC_instr is a fairly basic instruction screen.

PROC_menu allows the choice of three sub-programs, and jumps back to the control module so that the mode can be changed if necessary.

PROC_key prints a picture of the keyboard at the top of the screen.

PROC_learn contains the routine for letter position learning. **Line 1680** refers to the machine variable 'TIME' which counts up in centi-seconds time passed since the computer was switched on.

Line 1700 should probably be set to 30 or 50 to choose a reasonable amount of letters. You can leave it at 5 while you are testing the program.

Lines 1710–1760 choose and print a character on the screen. **Line 1720** defines a text window in the bottom half of the screen. If a command is now given to clear the screen with CLS, only this window is cleared.

Lines 1770–1820 check the input until the correct key is pressed. **Lines 1840–1890** read the value of 'TIME' again and calculate the number of seconds taken so far.

PROC_show checks to see if the key pressed is in one$, two$, etc. If it is, control jumps to PROC_print.

PROC_print prints the key in the correct position on the screen in colour 9, which flashes to show its position.

PROC_easy is the second stage — that of typing in easy words.

Lines 2130–2200 print the keyboard picture at the top of the screen. **Lines 2220–2270** allow the entry of the difficulty level from 1 to 5.

Line 2310 should have the value of 'go' increased when you have finished testing the program. **Lines 2320–2350** read words into word$. Only the last word read is displayed.

Lines 2390–2450 gets characters from the keyboard and prints them under the letters being copied. It continues to do this either until a mistake is made or the length of the word is reached. **Line 2460** either prints 'MISTAKE' or increases the score by one. **Lines 2490–2530** calculate the time taken as before.

PROC_hard is very similar to PROC_easy, and it would be possible to share the procedures if you were concerned at the overall length of the program. This would probably also reduce the clarity, however. The differences are mainly concerned with choosing a full sentence rather than single words.

Line 3000 onwards contain the words and sentences in data statements and can be altered as required. There should always be the right number of elements in the data lines when they are read from inside the program or else an 'out of data' error message will appear.

Note that lines like **line 2840** should be entered as one line — they only appear to be in three sections because of the formatting required to make 40 character listings appear neat.

Music

Electronics have revolutionised the music industry over the last few years, and it is now possible to copy many of the effects of the synthesiser on home computers. Acorn computers can produce a wide range of sounds, but the fact that they only have two statements to control all the effects can appear intimidating.

To discover the potential of your computer, it is useful to learn about the statements in easy stages. The more important of the two is SOUND. This controls the actual generation of the sound, whereas ENVELOPE shapes the sound. SOUND is followed by four parameters:

SOUND C,A,P,D

C is the channel selected and can have any value from 0 to 3, although on the Electron, 1 to 3 have the same effect and produce a square wave tone that is musical. If C is 0, a noise rather than a tone is generated.

A controls the amplitude or loudness, and also switches in any envelopes that have been selected. On the BBC, values from −1 to −15 act as a volume control, with −15 the loudest, but the Electron treats all negative values as the same volume. A value of 0 produces no sound. Positive values refer to the envelope number.

P controls the pitch; each increment of 1 produces a change in pitch of one eighth of a tone. The values can be any whole number from 0 to 255.

D controls the duration or length of the note and can be between 1 and 255. Each increment of one is equal to a duration of one twentieth of a second.

The ENVELOPE statement has 14 parameters, and alters the rather basic sounds generated by the SOUND statement. It can be viewed as a

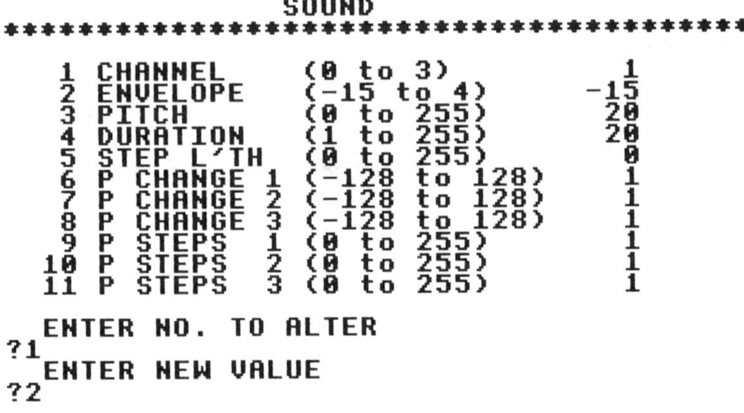

Figure 6.3: Screen Dump from Sound Demo.

sausage machine with the raw sound entering at one end and the 'sausage' of shaped sound leaving at the other. Sounds similar to those produced by commercial synthesisers can be produced by the BBC computer, but the Electron is deficient in some respects.

Out of the 14 parameters, only those controlling the pitch envelope actually have any effect on the Electron. The last five parameters, those that control the ADSR (attack, decay, sustain and release) are only included to match the superior control of the BBC. It is a shame that these are not implemented on the Electron, as they are more useful when it comes to 'impersonation' of musical instruments, etc.

So that you can experiment with different sounds, the following program allows you to alter all the parameters of both SOUND and ENVELOPE. It is designed to operate on both the Electron and BBC, so only those parameters that can change the sounds on both machines have been included. The last six numbers are

$$126,0,0,-126,126,126$$

to make the program compatible. If you wish to exploit the full potential of the BBC micro, it is simple to replace the constants in line 1480 with variables, and to include them at the input stage in PROC_main.

Sound Demo

```
1000 REM ***   SOUND DEMO   ***
1010 REM
1020 REM ***   AJS 2/2/84   ***
1025
1030 MODE6
1040 PROC_init
1050 REPEAT
1060    PROC_main
1070    UNTIL FALSE
1080
1090 DEFPROC_init
1100 VDU19,0,4;0;
1110 channel=1
1120 envelope=-15
1130 pitch=20
1140 duration=20
1150 Pi1=1
1160 Pi2=1
1170 Pi3=1
```

```
1180 Pr1=1
1190 Pr2=1
1200 Pr3=1
1210 steplen=0
1220 PRINTTAB(15,2)"SOUND"
1230 PRINTTAB(0,3)STRING$(40,"*")
1240 VDU28,0,24,39,5
1250 ENDPROC
1260
1270 DEFPROC_main
1280 @%=&00005
1290 PRINTTAB(2,0)
     " 1 CHANNEL     (0 to 3)      "
     channel
1300 PRINTTAB(2,1)
     " 2 ENVELOPE    (-15 to 4)    "
     envelope
1310 PRINTTAB(2,2)
     " 3 PITCH       (0 to 255)    "
     pitch
1320 PRINTTAB(2,3)
     " 4 DURATION    (1 to 255)    "
     duration
1330 PRINTTAB(2,4)
     " 5 STEP L'TH   (0 to 255)    "
     steplen
1340 PRINTTAB(2,5)
     " 6 P CHANGE 1 (-128 to 128)"Pi1
1350 PRINTTAB(2,6)
     " 7 P CHANGE 2 (-128 to 128)"Pi2
1360 PRINTTAB(2,7)
     " 8 P CHANGE 3 (-128 to 128)"Pi3
1370 PRINTTAB(2,8)
     " 9 P STEPS   1 (0 to 255)    "Pr1
1380 PRINTTAB(2,9)
     "10 P STEPS   2 (0 to 255)    "Pr2
1390 PRINTTAB(2,10)
     "11 P STEPS   3 (0 to 255)    "Pr3
1400 @%=10
1410 PROC_makesound
1420 PRINTTAB(2,12)"ENTER NO. TO ALTER"
1430 INPUT number
1440 PROC_change
1450 ENDPROC
```

```
1460
1470 DEFPROC_makesound
1480 ENVELOPE envelope,steplen,Pi1,Pi2,
     Pi3,Pr1,Pr2,Pr3,126,0,0,-126,126,
     126
1490 SOUND channel,envelope,pitch,
     duration
1500 ENDPROC
1510
1520 DEFPROC_change
1530 PRINTTAB(2,14)
     "ENTER NEW VALUE"
1540 INPUT value
1550 IF number = 1 AND value>=0
     AND value<4 THEN channel=value
1560 IF number = 2 AND value>= -15
     AND value<5 THEN envelope=value
1570 IF number = 3 AND value>=0
     AND value<256 THEN pitch=value
1580 IF number = 4 AND value>=1
     AND value<256 THEN duration=value
1590 IF number = 5 AND value>=0
     AND value<256 THEN steplen=value
1600 IF number = 6 AND value>= -128
     AND value<128 THEN Pi1=value
1610 IF number = 7 AND value>= -128
     AND value<128 THEN Pi2=value
1620 IF number = 8 AND value>= -128
     AND value<128 THEN Pi3=value
1630 IF number = 9 AND value>=0
     AND value<256 THEN Pr1=value
1640 IF number =10 AND value>=0
     AND value<256 THEN Pr2=value
1650 IF number =11 AND value>=0
     AND value<256 THEN Pr3=value
1660 CLS
1670 ENDPROC
```

Notes on the program

Lines 1030–1070 contain the control module.

PROC_init gives all the variables their initial values before they are altered by the user. **Line 1100** sets the background colour to blue.

The envelope variables follow the names given in the User Guide, so Pi1 is the number of steps in section one of the envelope.

Line 1240 defines a text window in which the display appears.

PROC_main controls the main display. **Line 1280** determines how the numeric variables are formatted on the screen. **Line 1400** resets the formatting to normal.

PROC_makesound plays the sound after setting the envelope values.

PROC_change keeps the size of the values within the required limits.

Storing tunes

Although the price of small synthesisers has fallen a great deal in the last few years, it is still useful to be able to turn your computer into a musical instrument when you wish. The last program gave you an idea of the many different sounds that can be achieved with SOUND and ENVELOPE. The final program in this chapter uses the SOUND statement to produce notes from a scale of nearly two octaves.

The keyboard of a computer is nothing like a piano keyboard, so this program attempts to link the sound of the note, a traditional keyboard and the written note on a piece of music. Many people find learning to read music difficult, so the program is designed to reinforce this learning stage by drawing a piano keyboard on the screen. At the same time as showing the note that is being played, it uses the capabilities of the Electron and BBC machines to produce the note which is then shown in its correct position on a stave at the top of the screen.

When music is used in programs, it is usual to store the pitch and duration of the notes in data statements at the end of the program. They can be read when necessary by use of RESTORE and READ. Here is a short demonstration of how you might achieve this.

Music in Data

```
1000 REM    **    MUSIC IN DATA     **
1010 REM
1020 REM    **    AJS 4/1/83        **
1030
1040 REPEAT
1050    RESTORE 1140
1060    FOR N = 1 TO 19
1070       READ pitch,duration
1080       SOUND 1,-15,pitch,duration
```

```
1090       NEXT N
1100     UNTIL FALSE
1110
1120 REM  ** CONGRATULATIONS! **
1130
1140 DATA 61,5,0,0,69,5,0,0,77,5,0,0,
     81,10,0,0,61,15,0,0,81,5,0,0,77,5,
     0,0,81,5,0,0,89,10,0,0,69,25
```

If you wished, you could alter the next program to play stored tunes in this manner, or even use the program to enter notes into an array. When a certain key was pressed, the tune could be replayed.

Figure 6.4: Screen Dump from Synth.

Meanwhile, on to the program itself, which should introduce to you a different way of reading the keyboard. Although it is fast enough for a simple monophonic synthesiser when run on an Electron, the BBC is much faster in mode 2 and it can give the impression of playing chords of up to three notes at the same time. Any other particular programming points are discussed in the notes after the program listing.

Synth

```
1000 REM   ***         SYNTH         ***
1010 REM
1020 REM   ***      AJS 4/4/83       ***
1030 REM
1040
1050 MODE1
1060 COLOUR129
1070 CLS
1080 PRINTTAB(15,2)"SYNTH"
1090 PRINTTAB(15,4)"*****"
1100 PRINTTAB(2,7)"USE THE ROW OF ";
     "THE KEYBOARD STARTING"
1110 PRINTTAB(4,9)"WITH CTRL AND ";
     "ENDING WITH RETURN"
1120 PRINTTAB(8,11)
     "AS THE NOTES OF A PIANO"
1130
1140 PRINTTAB(7,16)
     "PRESS SPACE BAR TO START"
1150 REPEAT
1160   Z$=GET$
1170   UNTILZ$=" "
1180
1190 MODE2
1200 PROC_init
1210 PROC_stave
1220 PROC_draw
1230 PROC_get
1240 STOP
1250
1260 DEFPROC_init
1270 VDU19,0,1;0;
1280 VDU19,1,0;0;
1290 VDU23,224,&7E,&7E,&7E,&7E,&7E,&7E,
     &7E,&7E
1300 VDU23,225,0,&42,0,&18,&18,0,&42,0
1310 scale$="CDEFGABCDEFGAB"
1320 black$="11011101101110"
1330 len%=255
1340 ENDPROC
1350
1360 DEFPROC_draw
```

```
1370  PRINTTAB(7,1)"SYNTH"
1380  VDU5
1390  GCOL0,7
1400  FORX=192TO1024STEP64
1410    FORY=320TO512STEP32
1420      MOVEX,Y
1430      PRINTCHR$224
1440      NEXTY
1450    NEXTX
1460  GCOL3,3
1470  FORX=192TO1088STEP64
1480    MOVEX,320
1490    PRINTMID$(scale$,X/64-2,1)
1500    NEXT
1510  GCOL0,1
1520  FORY=416TO542STEP32
1530    pos=1
1540    FORX=224TO1088STEP64
1550      MOVEX,Y
1560      IFMID$(black$,pos,1)="1"
          THENPRINTCHR$224
1570      pos=pos+1
1580      NEXTX
1590    NEXTY
1600  ENDPROC
1610
1620  DEFPROC_stave
1630  VDU24,400;600;850;900;
1640  GCOL0,135
1650  CLG
1660  VDU26
1670  GCOL0,0
1680  FORline=1TO5
1690    MOVE420,630+line*40
1700    PLOT1,420,0
1710    NEXT line
1720  MOVE640,870:PLOT1,60,0
1730  MOVE640,630:PLOT1,60,0
1740  GCOL0,1
1750  MOVE470,710
1760  FORN=1TO11
1770    READ X,Y
1780    DRAW X,Y
1790    NEXT N
```

```
1800 ENDPROC
1810
1820 DEFPROC_get
1830 REPEAT
1840    *FX12,1
1850    C1%=INKEY(-2)
1860    D1%=INKEY(-66)
1870    E1%=INKEY(-82)
1880    F1%=INKEY(-51)
1890    G1%=INKEY(-68)
1900    A1%=INKEY(-84)
1910    B1%=INKEY(-85)
1920    C2%=INKEY(-70)
1930    D2%=INKEY(-71)
1940    E2%=INKEY(-87)
1950    F2%=INKEY(-88)
1960    G2%=INKEY(-73)
1970    A2%=INKEY(-89)
1980    B2%=INKEY(-74)
1990    SP%=INKEY(-99)
2000    IFC1%=TRUE THEN SOUND
        &11,-15,53,len%:PROC_ping(1)
2010    IFD1%=TRUE THEN SOUND
        &11,-15,61,len%:PROC_ping(2)
2020    IFE1%=TRUE THEN SOUND
        &11,-15,69,len%:PROC_ping(3)
2030    IFF1%=TRUE THEN SOUND
        &11,-15,73,len%:PROC_ping(4)
2040    IFG1%=TRUE THEN SOUND
        &11,-15,81,len%:PROC_ping(5)
2050    IFA1%=TRUE THEN SOUND
        &11,-15,89,len%:PROC_ping(6)
2060    IFB1%=TRUE THEN SOUND
        &11,-15,97,len%:PROC_ping(7)
2070    IFC2%=TRUE THEN SOUND
        &11,-15,101,len%:PROC_ping(8)
2080    IFD2%=TRUE THEN SOUND
        &11,-15,109,len%:PROC_ping(9)
2090    IFE2%=TRUE THEN SOUND
        &11,-15,117,len%:PROC_ping(10)
2100    IFF2%=TRUE THEN SOUND
        &11,-15,121,len%:PROC_ping(11)
2110    IFG2%=TRUE THEN SOUND
        &11,-15,129,len%:PROC_ping(12)
```

```
2120    IFA2%=TRUE THEN SOUND
        &11,-15,137,len%:PROC_ping(13)
2130    IFB2%=TRUE THEN SOUND
        &11,-15,145,len%:PROC_ping(14)
2140    IFSP%=TRUE THEN SOUND
        &11,0,0,1
2150     UNTIL FALSE
2160
2170 DEFPROC_ping(X%)
2180 GCOL3,6
2190 MOVE640,625+X%*20
2200 PRINTCHR$111
2210 GCOL0,1
2220 MOVE128+(X%*64),352
2230 PRINTCHR$225
2240 MOVE128+(X%*64),352
2250 GCOL0,7
2260 PRINTCHR$224
2270 GCOL3,6
2280 MOVE640,625+X%*20
2290 PRINTCHR$111
2300 ENDPROC
2310
2320 REM *** DATA FOR TREBLE CLEF ***
2330
2340 DATA 460,725,480,740,520,710,470
2350 DATA 680,430,730,510,850,485,865
2360 DATA 470,850,510,630,480,615,460
2370 DATA 640
```

Notes on the program

Lines 1080–1140 contain the instructions. As they are only needed once, they are written at the start of the program.

Lines 1150–1170 repeat until the space bar is pressed. **Line 1190** selects mode 2, which allows a larger display. **Lines 1200–1230** set up the display. There could have been a REPEAT loop round PROC_get, but this program includes it in the procedure itself.

PROC_init sets up the foreground and background colours. **Lines 1290** and **1300** define two new characters, CHR$ 224 and CHR$ 225. **Lines 1310** and **1320** define strings to make the piano keyboard display easier to implement. **Line 1330** sets the length of the notes.

PROC_draw draws the piano keyboard. VDU5 is used to print text at the graphics cursor. The awkward numbers in the listing are simply those that fit the display on the screen in the best manner!

Lines 1400–1450 draw the white notes and label them. **Lines 1520–1590** draw the black notes. The string black$ is used to determine the positions of the black notes.

PROC_stave draws the stave in a graphics window at the top of the screen. **Line 1630** defines the position of this window. **Lines 1640** and **1650** change the colour of the window. **Lines 1680–1710** draw the lines. **Lines 1760–1790** read from data statements the instructions necessary to draw the treble clef.

PROC_get is used to scan the keyboard. **Line 1840** uses *FX12,1 to set the auto-repeat on the keys to its fastest setting.

Lines 1850–1990 check the middle row of keys to see if they are being pressed. If a key is pressed, it will return a value of -1, so its logic state is TRUE. If it is not pressed, it will return a value of 0, ie FALSE. The negative numbers in brackets are to identify which key you want to test. The full list is given in the User Guides for both the BBC and Electron machines in the keyword sections.

Lines 2000–2140 check if any variable is TRUE, ie set to -1 by the keyboard scan. If any are, a value according to the key pressed is passed to PROC_ping. **Line 2140** checks if the space bar has been pressed. All the other keys sound notes that carry on until they are switched off: the space bar does the switching off.

PROC_ping uses the variable X% to accept passed parameters that control the pitch of the note sounded. It also prints the note on the keyboard and on the stave. So that the note doesn't remain there, it is alternately plotted and replotted using exclusive OR plotting which makes it appear, then vanish. This is explained quite well in the Electron User Guide on page 154. Change the plotting statements from GCOL 3,6 to GCOL 0,6 to see the difference.

Lines 2340–2370 contain the data necessary to draw the treble clef.

CHAPTER 7
Program Design

Design philosophy

There has been a steady change in program writing philosophy over the past few years. With early forms of BASIC, it was necessary to compile long flowcharts before programming, and even these could often only partly help in deciphering the twistings and turnings of the program structure. Short programs did not often cause too much difficulty, but coming back to alter a program that had been written more than a few days previously would cause quite a few headaches. Sometimes a program would work, without the writer knowing exactly why.

BASIC has often been criticised because of these drawbacks. You have undoubtedly come across the notorious GOTO arguments. GOTO is a very useful command, and enables you to jump anywhere in a program, but it can make it difficult to understand if the flow of control darts all over the place. Due to arguments such as these, recent copies of BASIC have drawn upon other computer languages such as Pascal and BCPL for more precise control statements.

BBC BASIC has two loop structures, FOR–TO–NEXT and REPEAT–UNTIL. It does not have WHILE–ENDWHILE, which is a pity, and results in either more procedures than would otherwise be necessary or the use of GOTOs. FOR–TO–NEXT loops are fine when you know how many times you have to pass through the loop. REPEAT–UNTIL has advantages in that it can be used in situations where the number of loops is not known at the start. Also, the test to exit the loop is contained in the command UNTIL, so the structure is far neater. Because the test is at the end of the loop, however, it is necessary to go through the loop at least once, so WHILE would be preferred in some situations.

If you were writing a program to fill a bath, and the instructions were:

```
10 REPEAT
20 TURN ON TAPS
30 UNTIL BATH = FULL
```

then everything would be fine unless the bath was already full of water, in which case the floor would be bound to get rather damp. If you used DO WHILE, this would not happen:

```
10 WHILE BATH <> FULL
20 TURN ON TAPS
30 ENDWHILE
```

The difference between the two structures is that in the first, the test to end the loop is at the end, whereas in the second the test is at the start, and the loop will not be entered at all if the condition is false.

To get round the problem in BBC BASIC, you either use another procedure:

```
10 REPEAT
20 IF BATH <> FULL THEN PROC_TURNONTAPS
30 UNTIL BATH = FULL
```

or an implied GOTO:

```
10 REPEAT
20 IF BATH = FULL THEN 30 ELSE TURN ON TAPS
30 UNTIL BATH = FULL
```

However, this is a small price to pay when BBC BASIC contains so many other advantages such as the ability to use long variable names, like

name$ = "FRED" *and* cost = 6

Other BASICs allow this, but only recognise the first two letters in a variable name, so you could not use 'boatprice' and 'boatvalue' as two separate variables. Many BASICs are also choosy about which letters make up the variable name. If you try to use 'total' as a variable, the fact that it contains the word TO renders it unusable, as is the word 'Worthington', for the same reason — luckily, provided you keep to lower case variables, this does not happen with BBC BASIC.

BBC BASIC also has procedures which act as mini-programs, allowing the passing of parameters or values, and acting on them independently of the rest of the program.

In this book, I have tried where possible to make the flow of control fairly easy to understand by using long variable names and procedures, and by attempting to follow fairly sensible guidelines. I have found these a pleasant change after several years of programming on far less friendly languages than the one available on Acorn computers. These are by no means hard and fast regulations, merely suggestions that are intended to make it easier to concoct your own programs and perhaps to understand a little better what you have written.

Rule 1 seems very strange: turn off the computer. Although many ideas come to you at the keyboard, and short programs are easy to write at the keys, longer ones need a clear head, a pencil and paper. You need this to sketch out what you would like the program to do when it is completed. You can draw the screen displays, work out if a menu of choices is needed, and also the order in which things should proceed. It's very difficult to achieve these things sitting at the keyboard, and one advantage of this approach is that you don't even need a computer to carry out this stage.

The next step is to write out the control module. Using procedures, this is very simple, and can often show others what the program sets out to do in less than 30 lines.

As an example, I will imagine that I want a program to act as a notebook to record customer names and details of the type and value of goods they buy. The whole of the program can be contained in the control module as follows.

Stock

```
1000 REM ** CUSTOMER FILING SYSTEM **
1010 REM **         AJS   14/2/84      **
1020
1030 PROC_initiation
1040 MODE6
1050 VDU19,0,4;0;
1060 REPEAT
1070    PROC_menu
1080    UNTIL FALSE
1090
1100 DEFPROC_initiation
1110 DIM customer$(100)
1120 DIM address$(100)
1130 DIM product$(100)
1140 DIM stockval(100)
1150 N=0
1160 ENDPROC
1170
1180 DEFPROC_menu
1190 CLS
1200 PRINTTAB(10,1)"CUSTOMER FILE"
1210 PRINTTAB(0,3)STRING$(40,"*")
1220 PRINTTAB(2,5)"1 ENTER INFORMATION"
1230 PRINTTAB(2,7)"2 ALTER INFORMATION"
1240 PRINTTAB(2,9)"3 FIND CUSTOMER"
```

```
1250 PRINTTAB(2,11)"4 CHECK STOCK"
1260 PRINTTAB(2,13)"5 LOAD FILE"
1270 PRINTTAB(2,15)"6 SAVE FILE"
1280 PRINTTAB(2,17)"7 STOP"
1290 PRINT
1300 PRINT"CHOOSE A NUMBER"
1310 REPEAT
1320    Z$=GET$
1330    Z=VAL(Z$)
1340    UNTIL Z>0 AND Z<8
1350 IF Z=1 THEN PROC_enter
1360 IF Z=2 AND N>0 THEN PROC_change
1370 IF Z=3 AND N>0 THEN PROC_locate
1380 IF Z=4 AND N>0 THEN PROC_check
1390 IF Z=5 THEN PROC_load
1400 IF Z=6 AND N>0 THEN PROC_save
1410 IF Z=7 THEN STOP
1420 ENDPROC
1430
```

Note that I have included PROC_initiation before the menu, as this is only encountered once. Although the first time they are encountered, the computer reads procedures in order, their addresses are stored so that subsequent procedure calls take the same time whether they are at the beginning or end of a program. It does make the listing easier to read, however, if you put them in a logical order.

At this stage, the program has actually been written, as the whole of the control module is contained in PROC_menu. Now is the time to switch on and enter the program.

Program notes so far

PROC_initiation is used to set all initial values to zero, to dimension space for variable arrays, and to set colour values.

PROC_menu contains an initial display of options, and the user is invited to press a key.

GET$ is used to scan the keyboard and load the value of the key pressed into Z. The only keys that give results are those from 1 to 7 — all others, except ESCAPE and BREAK, are ignored. Notice that there is extra error-trapping here: you cannot branch to options that require data present until there is actually data in the program. This is achieved by testing to see if N (the number of customers) is greater than 1. Program control now branches to various procedures according to the value of Z. These all have names that show which job they perform.

Merging procedures

All that is necessary now is to write the mini-programs that make up the procedures. Some of these may be present in other programs that you have written previously, for instance, procedures to load and save files. This is how you can transfer a procedure from another program to this one.

First of all, check that you know the line numbers of the present program.

Next, load in the program that contains the procedure you need. Use DELETE to remove all the lines except those containing the procedure. Now use RENUMBER so that the line numbers do not conflict with those in the program you are writing. Type *SPOOL "proc" and then LIST the procedure. As you do this, you will be instructed to switch the tape recorder on to record an ASCII version of the program. Enter *SPOOL at the end, and then reload the original program. If you reposition the tape to the beginning and type *EXEC "proc", it will appear as if the procedure is being typed into the computer at high speed. At the end you will probably get a 'syntax error' message, but ignore it, as your program should now contain the procedure from the other program.

When you have merged all the procedures you can from tape or disk, those that need to be freshly written are entered. All procedures should have meaningful names, such as PROC_enter, or PROC_screen. You are not allowed to include spaces in the name, hence the dashes. It is fairly sensible to work on just one procedure at a time, as it can be tested without the rest of the program being written. It is clearly a lot easier to debug or correct a procedure than to tackle the whole program.

In the sample program, the most important procedure after the menu is the entry routine. So that each piece of information can be linked, all the data items entered at the same time are linked by number. If customer$(1) is FREDCO LTD, then address$(1) will contain the address of FREDCO, product$(1) will contain the product FREDCO use, and stockval contains the quantity or value of the product. This ensures that if you search for all the customers who buy crisps, for example, and if crisps are found in the product$ array at numbers 7, 8 and 23, then customer$ numbers 7, 8 and 23 will contain the names of those customers who buy crisps, and their details can be printed. Variable N holds the number of customers in the file at any time.

Here is the next procedure:

PROC_enter

```
1440 DEFPROC_enter
1450 N=N+1
1460 REPEAT
```

```
1470      CLS
1480      PRINTTAB(14,1)"DATA INPUT"
1490      PRINTTAB(0,3)STRING$(40,"*")
1500      PRINTTAB(2,5)"(NO COMMAS)"
1510      PRINTTAB(2,7)"ENTER CUSTOMER"
1520      INPUTTAB(2,9)customer$(N)
1530      PRINTTAB(2,11)"ENTER ADDRESS"
1540      INPUTTAB(2,13)address$(N)
1550      PRINTTAB(2,15)"ENTER PRODUCT"
1560      INPUTTAB(2,17)product$(N)
1570      PRINTTAB(2,19)"ENTER AMOUNT"
1580      INPUTTAB(2,21)stockval(N)
1590      PRINTTAB(2,23)"IS THIS CORRECT?"
1600      Z$=GET$
1610      UNTIL Z$="Y"
1620 ENDPROC
1630
```

Notes

This procedure should be fairly self-explanatory. The number N is incremented (or increased) by 1, and the customer name, address, product and value are entered into the array. At the end, you are asked if the data entered is correct. If it is, the REPEAT–UNTIL loop is only used once.

Once the data is in the memory, you might wish to alter it, particularly the stock values. This is achieved in the next procedure, PROC_change.

PROC_change

```
1640 DEFPROC_change
1650 CLS
1660 PRINTTAB(10,1)"CHANGE INFORMATION"
1670 PRINTTAB(0,3)STRING$(40,"*")
1680 PRINTTAB(2,5)"ENTER CUSTOMER NAME"
1690 INPUTTAB(2,7)search$
1700 FOR X=1 TO N
1710    found=0
1720    IF LEN(search$) >
        LEN(customer$(N)) THEN 1750
1730    find=INSTR(customer$(X),search$)
1740    IF find <>0 THEN PROC_found
1750    NEXT X
1760 ENDPROC
1770
```

Notes

The screen is cleared, and the display title entered as in all the procedures by using the STRING$ function. Instead of stating

PRINT "*****"

you can say

PRINT STRING$(5,"*")

This is obviously only easier to use when long strings are employed, as in the example in the program, all across the screen.

This procedure uses the INSTR function to test if there is an occurrence of the search string in the array of customer names. If you cannot remember the whole name, just part of it can be entered. For example, if you knew you had to change the address of a customer whose name ended in 'SON', then using SON as the search string would find all customers with this series of letters somewhere in their names.

The rather untidy line that checks on the comparative lengths of search and customer strings (line 1720) is only necessary for those people who are using this program on a BBC computer with series 1.0 and 1.2 operating systems. Indeed, not even all of these machines were affected. There is an infrequently-mentioned bug that crashes the computer if you use INSTR without protecting it. Normally INSTR returns the first position of the second string in the first, eg:

X = INSTR("ABRACADABRA", "ABRA")

This will give X the value of 1, as that is the position of ABRA inside the long string. If, however, the second string is longer than the first, then instead of a value of 0 being returned, as should happen, curious things occur.

X = INSTR("ABC","ABCDEF")

will corrupt the stack (the pile of return addresses used by the computer) and not only will you get a strange error message with no line number and peculiar graphic symbols flashing on the screen, you also stand a good chance of losing the program completely and having to start again from scratch.

In this procedure, if the string is found, control jumps to PROC_found.

PROC_found

```
1780 DEFPROC_found
1790 CLS
1800 PRINTTAB(10,1)"CHANGE INFORMATION"
1810 PRINTTAB(0,3)STRING$(40,"*")
1820 PRINTTAB(2,5)"CUSTOMER NAME"
1830 PRINTTAB(4,7)customer$(X)
1840 PRINTTAB(2,9)"DATA STORED:-"
1850 PRINTTAB(4,11)address$(X)
1860 PRINTTAB(4,13)product$(X)
1870 PRINTTAB(4,15)stockval(X)
1880 PRINTTAB(2,17)
        "DO YOU WISH TO CHANGE ANYTHING?"
1890 Z$=GET$
1900 IF Z$="N" THEN ENDPROC
1910 PRINTTAB(2,19)
        "ADD'SS(A), PROD(P), OR AM'NT(V)?"
1920 REPEAT
1930    Z$=GET$
1940    UNTIL Z$="A" OR Z$="P" OR Z$="V"
1950 IF Z$="A"THEN INPUTTAB(2)
        "ENTER NEW ADDRESS" ' address$(X)
1960 IF Z$="P"THEN INPUTTAB(2)
        "ENTER NEW PRODUCT" ' product$(X)
1970 IF Z$="V"THEN INPUTTAB(2)
        "ENTER NEW AMOUNT" ' stockval(X)
1980 ENDPROC
1990
```

Notes

PROC_found prints a display of all the information you have on the selected customers. It then allows you to change any of the details by altering the relevant section of the arrays. Notice that there is the option of not altering anything, which is an important choice. Immediately <RETURN> is pressed, control jumps back to PROC_change in case anything else needs to be altered.

The next procedure is similar to the last, in its use of search routines using INSTR, but it gives far more options.

PROC_locate

```
2000 DEFPROC_locate
2010 LOCAL Z
```

```
2020 CLS
2030 PRINTTAB(10,2)"FIND CUSTOMER"
2040 PRINTTAB(0,3)STRING$(40,"*")
2050 PRINTTAB(2,5)
     "1 SEARCH CUSTOMER NAME"
2060 PRINTTAB(2,7)
     "2 SEARCH CUSTOMER ADDRESS"
2070 PRINTTAB(2,9)
     "3 SEARCH PRODUCT"
2080 PRINTTAB(2,11)
     "4 RETURN TO MAIN MENU"
2090 PRINTTAB(2,13)
     "CHOOSE OPTION"
2100 REPEAT
2110    Z$=GET$
2120    Z=VAL(Z$)
2130    UNTIL Z>0 AND Z<5
2140 PRINTTAB(2,15)
     "ENTER SEARCH STRING"
2150 INPUTTAB(2,17)search$
2160 FOR X=1 TO N
2170    found=0
2180    IF Z=1 AND LEN(search$) >
        LEN(customer$(X)) THEN 2250
2190    IF Z=2 AND LEN(search$) >
        LEN(address$(X)) THEN 2250
2200    IF Z=3 AND LEN(search$) >
        LEN(product$(X)) THEN 2250
2210    IF Z=1 THEN found =
        INSTR(customer$(X),search$)
2220    IF Z=2 THEN found =
        INSTR(address$(X),search$)
2230    IF Z=3 THEN found =
        INSTR(product$(X),search$)
2240    IF found<>0 THEN PROC_display
2250    NEXT X
2260 ENDPROC
2270
```

Notes

After the title appears, another menu is shown that gives you the opportunity to search for customers according to the different information you may have. If you know the name, all entries under that will be shown. If you know the address, all customers at a particular address will be shown. This is a useful aspect of using INSTR, as you can use LONDON as a search string, and all customers in London will appear. Notice that you have to be careful with this facility, as any customer with an address in LONDON ST, ANYTOWN will also be shown. To prevent this, you could dimension a separate array called town$(X) to hold the towns, but that will increase the complexity and decrease the memory space.

If you want to display all those customers who buy crisps, then you can enter CRISPS as the search string, but you could easily include code letters to show, for instance, perishable goods by prefixing the product by a 'P/'. Notice the use of another REPEAT–UNTIL loop to make sure that only the menu choices offered (variable Z) can be chosen.

PROC_display follows on from the present procedure to show all the data selected by the program and contains a simple display routine.

PROC_display

```
2280  DEFPROC_display
2290  CLS
2300  PRINTTAB(10,1)
      "INFORMATION STORED:-"
2310  PRINTTAB(0,3)STRING$(40,"*")
2320  PRINTTAB(2,5) "CUSTOMER NAME:-"
2330  PRINTTAB(4,7)customer$(X)
2340  PRINTTAB(2,9) "ADDRESS:-"
2350  PRINTTAB(4,11)address$(X)
2360  PRINTTAB(2,13) "PRODUCT:-"
2370  PRINTTAB(4,15)product$(X)
2380  PRINTTAB(2,17) "AMOUNT:-"
2390  PRINTTAB(4,19)stockval(X)
2400  PRINTTAB(2,21)
      "PRESS SPACE BAR TO CONTINUE"
2410  Z$=GET$
2420  ENDPROC
2430
```

Notes
This is similar to PROC_found and should be fairly clear. PROC_check is rather more elaborate.

PROC_check

```
2440  DEFPROC_check
2450  total=0
2460  CLS
2470  PRINTTAB(10,2)"CHECK STOCK LEVEL"
2480  PRINTTAB(0,3)STRING$(40,"*")
2490  PRINTTAB(2,5)"ENTER THE PRODUCT:-"
2500  INPUTsearchprod$
2510  @%=&20209
2520  FOR X=1 TO N
2530     found=0
2540     IF LEN(searchprod$) >
         LEN(product$(X)) THEN 2580
2550     found =
         INSTR(product$(X),searchprod$)
2560     IF found<>0 THEN total =
         total+stockval(X)
2570     IF found<>0 THEN PRINT
         customer$(X)TAB(15)product$(X)
         TAB(30)stockval(X)
2580     NEXT X
2590  PRINT
2600  PRINTTAB(2)"TOTAL AMOUNT OF ";
      searchprod$;" = ";total
2610  @%=&10
2620  PRINTTAB(2,21)
      "PRESS SPACE BAR TO CONTINUE"
2630  Z$=GET$
2640  ENDPROC
2650
```

Notes

This procedure is used to find out the total value of any particular product and this too makes use of the INSTR function. It has been designed to check the stock purchased by all customers and it has been deliberately left in a flexible form for easy modification. At the entry stage, instructions could be added so that the amount of stock can be entered, or the value, or the weight, indeed any numerical value to go into the array stockval.

After the search string searchprod$ has been entered, the numeric display is altered by the line that says

@%=&20209

This forces all numbers to be printed in a particular format consisting of two decimal places and a field width of nine characters. What you will notice in real terms is that any decimal points appear neatly underneath each other in the display, and any extra decimal places are rounded off. This formatting is returned to normal by the line

@%=&10

as otherwise all numbers following appear with two decimal places, which can look a little strange.

Although the purpose of the INSTR function is to let you know the position of the search string in the string being tested, this feature is not used. Any occurrence results in a value other than 0, and the details are printed on the screen. The variable 'total' is used to store the cumulative total of all the stockvals that are found. This routine is so versatile that if you were, say, a grocer and used this to store your stock of vegetables, then a search string of PEA would find the value of all peas from all customers, whether they were entered as PROCESSED PEAS or SWEET PEAS. You would have to be careful that you didn't have any PEACHES in there, however, as they would be included too. This is why a routine to print all products chosen has been included, so you can see which values have been added together to produce the total.

As the last line is a print statement and not an input, you have to press a key to get back to the menu. To make the design easier, even though the instructions say 'PRESS SPACE BAR', the input is not checked, and any key will suffice.

At this stage, it is useful to be able to load and save data that has been entered into the program, so these operations are achieved by PROC_save and PROC_load. The next two routines should be very familiar, and are similar to most of the save/load routines in this book. Although the initialisation has set the size of the file to 100 customers, there is enough room in the memory for considerably more, although if you add too many arrays for other information, the total may drop. If this happens, you could divide up your customers into two or more categories, and store them on separate files.

PROC_load and PROC_save

```
2660 DEFPROC_load
2670 CLS
2680 PRINTTAB(10,1)"LOADING FILE"
2690 PRINTTAB(0,3)STRING$(40,"*")
```

```
2700 PRINTTAB(2,5)
     "ENTER THE NAME OF THE FILE"
2710 INPUTTAB(2,7)file$
2720 z%=OPENIN(file$)
2730 PRINTTAB(2,9)"FOUND "file$
2740 INPUT#z%,N
2750 FOR X=1 TO N
2760    INPUT#z%,customer$(X)
2770    INPUT#z%,address$(X)
2780    INPUT#z%,product$(X)
2790    INPUT#z%,stockval(X)
2800    NEXT X
2810 CLOSE#z%
2820 ENDPROC
2830
2840 DEFPROC_save
2850 CLS
2860 PRINTTAB(10,1)"SAVING FILE"
2870 PRINTTAB(0,3)STRING$(40,"*")
2880 PRINTTAB(2,5)
     "ENTER THE NAME OF THE FILE"
2890 INPUTTAB(2,7)file$
2900 PRINTTAB(2,9)"SAVING "file$
2910 z%=OPENOUT(file$)
2920 PRINT#z%,N
2930 FOR X=1 TO N
2940    PRINT#z%,customer$(X)
2950    PRINT#z%,address$(X)
2960    PRINT#z%,product$(X)
2970    PRINT#z%,stockval(X)
2980    NEXT X
2990 CLOSE#z%
3000 ENDPROC
```

Notes

The screen format is the same as the other procedures. In PROC_save
you are given the opportunity to name the file, and an output channel
is opened. The information written to the file is the number of entries,
N, and the contents of the four arrays, customer$(X), address$(X),
product$(X) and stockval (X). The number, N, is used to control the size
of the loop, and the file is then closed.

  To load data via PROC_load, the procedure is very similar to

PROC_save. This time, the file name is entered, a channel opened, and the file loaded into memory.

Although these two procedures come at the end of the listing, it is often a good idea to put rudimentary save/load routines in early on during the development of the program, simply to save time entering test data to see if the other procedures act correctly. When the program reaches this stage, it needs to be tested to see if you have covered all possible eventualities.

If you have a printer, you may also want to incorporate routines to print out various results. This is quite simple, as there are VDU commands to do this for you. Add the line VDU2 when you want data to be directed to the printer as well as to the screen, VDU1 if you only want output at the printer, and VDU3 when you wish to turn the printer output off.

Next comes the job of modification and error-trapping. One important consideration is whether you allow users to input names in lower case as well as upper case. It is simpler to manage if only upper case is used, but perhaps this should be stated at the start of the program. If you enter a word when a figure was requested, does the program give an error message and stop? What happens when you run out of memory? What happens when you run out of dimensioned array space? (This will happen when you reach more than 100 entries in the present program.) Perhaps you need to enter more information, or the program doesn't show you what you need to know, so it needs to be modified. If you have designed it methodically, it should not present too many difficulties when you come to do this.

Lastly, before you commit your valuable business records to the new program, get some of your friends to try it out. You can use it a hundred times without discovering anything wrong, when a fresh uscr can find bugs straight away.

Index

Program names are in italics.

Other titles from Sunshine

SPECTRUM BOOKS

Artificial Intelligence on the Spectrum Computer
Keith & Steven Brain   ISBN 0 946408 37 8   **£6.95**
Spectrum Adventures
Tony Bridge & Roy Carnell   ISBN 0 946408 07 6   **£5.95**
Machine Code Sprites and Graphics for the ZX Spectrum
John Durst   ISBN 0 946408 51 3   **£6.95**
ZX Spectrum Astronomy
Maurice Gavin   ISBN 0 946408 24 6   **£6.95**
Spectrum Machine Code Applications
David Laine   ISBN 0 946408 17 3   **£6.95**
The Working Spectrum
David Lawrence   ISBN 0 946408 00 9   **£5.95**
Inside Your Spectrum
Jeff Naylor & Diane Rogers   ISBN 0 946408 35 1   **£6.95**
Master your ZX Microdrive
Andrew Pennell   ISBN 0 946408 19 X   **£6.95**

COMMODORE 64 BOOKS

Graphic Art for the Commodore 64
Boris Allan   ISBN 0 946408 15 7   **£5.95**
DIY Robotics and Sensors on the Commodore Computer
John Billingsley   ISBN 0 946408 30 0   **£6.95**
Artificial Intelligence on the Commodore 64
Keith & Steven Brain   ISBN 0 946408 29 7   **£6.95**
Simulation Techniques on the Commodore 64
John Cochrane   ISBN 0 946408 58 0   **£6.95**
Machine Code Graphics and Sound for the Commodore 64
Mark England & David Lawrence   ISBN 0 946408 28 9   **£6.95**
Commodore 64 Adventures
Mike Grace   ISBN 0 946408 11 4   **£5.95**
Business Applications for the Commodore 64
James Hall   ISBN 0 946408 12 2   **£5.95**
Mathematics on the Commodore 64
Czes Kosniowski   ISBN 0 946408 14 9   **£5.95**
Advanced Programming Techniques on the Commodore 64
David Lawrence   ISBN 0 946408 23 8   **£5.95**

Commodore 64 Disk Companion
David Lawrence & Mark England   ISBN 0 946408 49 1   £7.95
The Working Commodore 64
David Lawrence   ISBN 0 946408 02 5   £5.95
Commodore 64 Machine Code Master
David Lawrence & Mark England   ISBN 0 946408 05 X   £6.95
Machine Code Games Routines for the Commodore 64
Paul Roper   ISBN 0 946408 47 5   £6.95
Programming for Education on the Commodore 64
John Scriven & Patrick Hall   ISBN 0 946408 27 0   £5.95
Writing Strategy Games on your Commodore 64
John White   ISBN 0 946408 54 8   £6.95

COMMODORE PLUS/4 & C16 BOOKS

The Working C16
David Lawrence   ISBN 0 946408 62 9   £6.95

ELECTRON BOOKS

Graphic Art for the Electron Computer
Boris Allan   ISBN 0 946408 20 3   £5.95
Programming for Education on the Electron Computer
John Scriven & Patrick Hall   ISBN 0 946408 21 1   £5.95

BBC COMPUTER BOOKS

Functional Forth for the BBC Computer
Boris Allan   ISBN 0 946408 04 1   £5.95
Graphic Art for the BBC Computer
Boris Allan   ISBN 0 946408 08 4   £5.95
DIY Robotics and Sensors for the BBC Computer
John Billingsley   ISBN 0 946408 13 0   £6.95
Artificial Intelligence on the BBC and Electron
Keith & Steven Brain   ISBN 0 946408 36 X   £6.95
Essential Maths on the BBC and Electron Computer
Czes Kosniowski   ISBN 0 946408 34 3   £5.95
Programming for Education on the BBC Computer
John Scriven & Patrick Hall   ISBN 0 946408 10 6   £5.95
Making Music on the BBC Computer
Ian Waugh   ISBN 0 946408 26 2   £5.95

Sunshine also publishes

POPULAR COMPUTING WEEKLY

The first weekly magazine for home computer users. Each copy contains Top 10 charts of the best-selling software and books and up-to-the-minute details of the latest games. Other features in the magazine include regular hardware and software reviews, programming hints, computer swap, adventure corner and pages of listings for the Spectrum, Dragon, BBC, VIC 20 and 64, ZX 81 and other popular micros. Only 40p a week, a year's subscription costs £19.95 (£9.98 for six months) in the UK and £37.40 (£18.70 for six months) overseas.

DRAGON USER

The monthly magazine for all users of Dragon microcomputers. Each issue contains reviews of software and peripherals, programming advice for beginners and advanced users, program listings, a technical advisory service and all the latest news related to the Dragon. A year's subscription (12 issues) costs £10 in the UK and £16 overseas.

MICRO ADVENTURER

The monthly magazine for everyone interested in Adventure games, war gaming and simulation/role-playing games. Includes reviews of all the latest software, lists of all the software available and programming advice. A year's subscription (12 issues) costs £10 in the UK and £16 overseas.

COMMODORE HORIZONS

The monthly magazine for all users of Commodore computers. Each issue contains reviews of software and peripherals, programming advice for beginners and advanced users, program listings, a technical advisory service and all the latest news. A year's subscription costs £10 in the UK and £16 overseas.

For further information contact:
Sunshine
12–13 Little Newport Street
London WC2R 3LD
01-437 4343

Telex: 296275

NOTES

NOTES

NOTES

NOTES

NOTES

NOTES

NOTES